THE NEWLY FRUGAL

THE NEWLY FRUGAL

A Beginner's Guide to the Frugal Lifestyle

Lindsay Ripplinger

songbird
PUBLISHING

Published by Songbird Publishing

10 9 8 7 6 5 4 3 2 1

For my mom,

who showed me that true wealth is measured not in money, but in wisdom, resourcefulness, and heart.

Thank you for teaching me frugality by living it, sharing your journey, and inspiring me every day to find joy in what truly matters.

Table of Contents

Introduction

I'm a born-and-raised frugarian. A *frugarian* is what I like to call a person who has fully embraced the frugal lifestyle. In my early childhood, we were a conventional family. My mom stayed home and took care of the kids while my dad worked. It was the traditional dynamic of provider and homemaker. This structure allowed my mom time to bake loaves of bread from scratch each morning, to sew and make some of our clothes, and to cook hearty prairie meals with simple, nourishing ingredients. It also fostered an environment of learning and gave us kids the chance to absorb the techniques we needed to be self-sufficient adults—adults who not only understand the value of money but also how much easier it is to save than earn.

In elementary school, my parents separated, and my mom was faced with raising two daughters on a single income. She was just at the beginning of her professional career, and money was extremely tight. Fortunately, as a born-and-raised frugarian herself, she took the change in stride and implemented some of the more advanced frugal techniques outlined in this book to help our family survive. From an early age, I understood the difference between needs and wants, as well as the value of experiences over more *stuff*.

By junior high, arguably the toughest time in a young girl's life, I already had years of frugal living experience. I was starting to see the value in setting small financial goals, earning money through part-time jobs, and learning to embrace the freedom that comes from ignoring the expectations of others. I looked at thrift stores as a game and developed my own simple sense of style based on the clothing I could buy from the rummage bin at Sally Ann.

The grunge era was in full swing by the time I reached high school, and there was also a resurgence of the vintage and retro aesthetic. Activities with my friends often revolved around trips to the thrift store, where we would challenge each other to see who could get the coolest-looking outfit for the least amount of money. Whenever one of us was complimented on something we thrifted, we beamed with satisfaction knowing the fractional amount we spent. Since none of us had much money, it was also a time of social gatherings in the home—watching movies, singing karaoke, or completing jigsaw puzzles while listening to music.

I lived at home until I started college in the fall after high school, and the transition from dependency to self-sufficiency was relatively easy. I had been taught how to budget, how to shop for deals, how to cook, and how to avoid extending myself beyond what I could afford. I was by no means perfect, and I even fell into the common college trap of shopping, partying, and eating copious quantities of expensive junk food. I also learned a hard lesson after a pushy salesman at a big box store signed me up for a credit card. I was sold the promise of easy money without fully understanding the impacts of 28% interest.

Once I experienced the weight of debt—whether from that credit card or the $88,000 in student loans I graduated with—I knew it was a situation I wanted to escape from and never be bound by again. I started my post-college career in an incredibly low-paying mailroom job and rented a studio suite in a boarding house with seven other people. I shared a bathroom down the hall and a washer and dryer in the basement. I made do with a $25-per-week food budget because it was all I could afford.

My income slowly increased over the following decade, but I lived like a student for as long as I could. I cooked at home, avoided lifestyle inflation, and put every spare dollar toward paying down what I owed. My frugality allowed me to discharge my debt in eight years instead of the scheduled fifteen, freeing me from the constant stress of owing money. That experience taught me discipline and the peace that comes from living below my means. Now, I'm excited to share my knowledge and experience with others looking to adopt the frugal lifestyle for themselves.

This book is a testament to the power of frugality and the strength that comes from self-sufficiency. It shows that even through difficult challenges, such as being a single mother, losing a job, or putting yourself through college, goals can be accomplished through planning, sacrifice, and gratitude. Being frugal is much more than being a penny-pincher—it's about understanding where life's true values lie: in relationships, community, and experiences.

Part 1
Frugal First Steps

What is Frugality?

Frugality isn't just about saving money—it's a way of thinking about what you really need to survive and thrive. Frugarians tend to focus less on what they *want* and more on what they *need*. Frugality is a way of living that's based on the ideals of making do with what you have and being grateful for it. It's being mindful about how you spend your money and considering carefully before you part with it. Saving money as part of a frugal lifestyle isn't just the focus—it's a natural by-product.

At its core, frugality is a way of functioning with as few resources as possible. In the typical North American lifestyle, part of the "American Dream" is to accumulate as much stuff as possible, and then prove to others that you have been successful by showing off that stuff. This could mean wearing the latest fashions, dining out multiple times per week, or going on expensive holidays. It could mean a massive McMansion with more square footage than you'll ever use in your day-to-day living, or luxury cars that you barely have time to drive because of the high-pressure careers required to afford them. Frugality, on the other hand, means stripping your life down to the ultimate essentials and rebuilding it based on what you need to bring true joy to your life—while ignoring the expectations of others who are often in debt up to their ears.

Being frugal also means understanding effort and valuing time. It's taking stock of the energy that goes into earning money and striving to get as much value as possible from what you spend. Frugality also means being mindful of waste—it's not throwing something away if it still has a purpose, and it's buying quality items so they last longer relative to the price paid.

As you begin to consider more deeply the effort behind earning every dollar, your sense of value starts to shift. Take new shoes, for example. Buying a low-quality pair for $40 that wears out in six months isn't very frugal. A frugarian might wonder, "If I spent $120 on a higher-quality pair, could I get a year and a half or more of wear?" Not only would you enjoy better comfort over that time, but you'd also save money and effort in other ways—fewer trips to the store, less gas spent, and fewer impulse purchases along the way.

Adopting a frugal lifestyle can help you better understand where life's true fulfillment comes from. It's not about surrounding yourself with consumer goods. It's about meeting your needs in the most economical way possible, while focusing your time and energy on nurturing relationships, enjoying moments with family and friends, and building a strong community of like-minded people around you.

Pre-Frugal Self-Assessment

Before you dig into the work of building your frugal foundations, a pre-frugal self-assessment is a chance to take stock of any frugal habits or behaviours you already have. As a new frugarian, it's useful to acknowledge the frugal things you're already doing and reinforce your ability to lead a frugal lifestyle. You may find it helpful to keep a journal or notebook so you can identify your goals and refer back to them later. It's also handy to have a central place where you can jot down frugal tips and tricks or note aspects of the lifestyle that you may be struggling with—or want to learn more about.

Consider whether you know anyone who leads a frugal lifestyle. It can be really beneficial to speak with people who are already living frugally. Most frugarians are eager to share their experiences and offer sage advice to newcomers. I know I get excited when friends ask me about my frugality. It feels like a chance to share a bit of knowledge, and maybe even a bit of wisdom. It's also a great feeling when you later learn that those same friends have adopted a frugal lifestyle or that aspects of their frugal journey have been positive. So, keep an ear open—there are a ton of frugarians out there.

In your notebook, write down any frugal habits you already have. Do you swish your shampoo bottle with water when it gets really low to squeeze out a few more washes? Do you hang your laundry on the line in the summer because you love the fresh scent it gives your clothes? Do you do your own oil changes instead of taking your car to the shop? I'll bet you have more frugal habits than you think!

Levels of Frugality
Occasionally Frugal

The *occasionally frugal* person may have learned frugal habits over the years, but those behaviours aren't an ingrained part of their life. They'll take opportunities to be frugal if they come up naturally, but may not be willing to change their lifestyle to seek them out. They might buy the occasional piece of clothing at a thrift store, save their butter tubs for later use, or walk a few blocks to the corner store instead of driving—but they also see no issue with spending money on items they want and may even carry debt to do so.

Faithfully Frugal

The *faithfully frugal* person has fully adopted the frugal lifestyle. Frugality is so ingrained in their daily life that it becomes second nature. They view every purchase through the lens of frugality and assess their wants and needs to determine whether the expense is necessary. If they purchase a "want" item, they ponder it before buying and never go into debt to make the purchase. They see the value in quality, live a life of minimalism, and strive to teach others about the frugal lifestyle. Their friendships and relationships are often with others who share similar ideals.

Extremely Frugal

The *extremely frugal* person is faithful to the frugal lifestyle but takes measures that others may view as over the top. This may include foraging for food in city parks, dumpster diving, or only using items that they can get for free. They may forgo the use of a car altogether and rely instead on walking, biking, or public transportation. They may not have internet or a phone, and prefer to use the services of the library for their communication needs. They rarely spend money unnecessarily and avoid many (if any) entertainment activities that aren't free.

The main thread that ties all three types of frugarians together is the degree to which they will go to satisfy their wants and needs. The key difference between a want and a need is simple: a *need* is something required to meet the basic requirements of life in modern society, such as food, shelter, clothing, water, transportation, and utilities. A *want* is something that is nice to have but is not necessary for survival. This distinction may vary based on your circumstances, but it should be fairly easy for you to differentiate between items you purchase to fulfill a basic human need and those you buy because you feel like it.

Frugal vs. Cheap

There's a common misconception that being frugal is the same as being cheap. While both involve a desire to save money, the motivations behind the two are quite different. Being cheap is often looked down upon because the person is doing so without considering the cost or consequences of their cheapness. A good example is a cheap person going out for dinner, receiving exceptional service, enjoying their meal, but not leaving a tip. Their cheapness comes at a cost to the server because they are not being generous or gracious in receiving that service. They focus only on what they will gain by denying the money to someone else.

A frugarian, on the other hand, may see dining out as a want rather than a need. They could have spent the time at home with loved ones, connecting over a frugal home-cooked meal. Instead, going to a restaurant is viewed as a special occasion. The experience is out of the ordinary and, as a result, inherently joyful. They may engage with their server, enjoy the restaurant's ambiance, and savour the food. At the end of the meal, they may offer a gracious "thank you" and leave an appropriate tip because the motivation behind their experience is different.

Motivation

For many frugarians, frugality is born out of necessity. As in the example of my mom, even though she was raised by parents who lived through the Great Depression and was reared with her four siblings on a bus driver's salary, it wasn't until she was a single mother and faced with no other option that frugality became the mainstay of her life.

Adopting a frugal lifestyle isn't something to be taken lightly—it's rarely a way of living that people come to without some kind of inspiration behind it. For the newly frugal, motivations can range from saving money after a job loss to achieving a large financial goal, like buying a home or funding a child's education. When you think about your reasons for becoming frugal, consider your life in its current state. What about the way you live now, and how you spend and save your money, is causing you to consider this lifestyle? By understanding why you want to become frugal, it will be easier to take the necessary steps toward it.

The Forced Frugarian

A *forced frugarian* is someone who is living the frugal lifestyle because they have no other option. This doesn't necessarily mean they don't want to be living frugally, but rather that they don't have the financial means to live any other way. Forced frugality can be the result of a job loss or divorce, an unexpected medical expense, or even an increased cost of living in your area.

I know that change isn't easy, particularly when you didn't choose this direction for your life. But I want you to understand that frugality isn't a prison sentence. For many forced frugarians, the end result of long-term frugality is much more freedom. By focusing on what's truly important in your life, you'll see that you don't have to be defined by your circumstances. With each day living the frugal lifestyle, your motivation to continue will grow, and you'll be empowered by your ability to consistently provide the basic needs for yourself and your family.

The Born-and-Raised Frugarian

Personally, I fall into the *born-and-raised frugarian* category. As a result of my mom's forced frugality, the frugal lifestyle has been all I've ever known. In my family, we learned to make do with what we had but also understood that, in doing so, we could afford an occasional indulgence. It has been 35 years, and I still fondly remember my fifth-grade birthday when my mom took four friends and me to an amusement park to celebrate. Even though it was expensive, she could afford it because of her "fun fund" that she dipped into for special occasions.

Through hands-on experience, the frugal lifestyle becomes natural. A born-and-raised frugarian may have seen their dad working on the budget in the evening to make sure that all of the fixed expenses for the month were taken care of. They may have seen their mom sitting at the kitchen table, mending the frayed cuff on a pair of jeans or cleaning the finer details of a pair of sneakers with a toothbrush. Frugality was all around, and many of us hold onto those habits in adulthood.

One of the teachings from my mom that I'm most grateful for is that she never framed frugality negatively—it was always a positive action to be thankful for. She still views the lifestyle as a game: how inexpensively she can get something she needs and how long she can make it last. Even when she indulges in a want, she loves the challenge of getting it for the least amount of money. These lessons often pass from generation to generation—great-great-grandparents who settled the West, great-grandparents who fought in world wars, grandparents who survived the Great Depression, and their children who rallied during the devastating recession of the 1980s. Even today, many people are still dealing with the economic impacts of the pandemic. The learnings from each of these trials can be passed on to the next generation simply through living each day frugally.

The Debt Prisoner

There's a distinction between individuals who are in debt as a result of their needs (such as a medical expense) and those who don't understand the value of money and buy everything on credit. When I refer to the *debt prisoner*, I mean those people with the "buy-now-pay-later" mentality. When you're a prisoner to debt, you have fallen into the trap of consumerism—placing a much higher value on the things you want while failing to recognize the simplicity of your needs. Debt prisoners are often trapped by expectations and the compulsion to "Keep up with the Joneses"—whether they can afford to or not. They may not understand the concept of a budget or how to create and stick to one.

While born-and-raised frugarians often learn the principles of mindful spending early in life, others grow up with different experiences and expectations around money. Some people weren't taught how to distinguish wants from needs or how to connect spending money with the time and effort it takes to earn. This is incredibly common in North America, where cultural narratives like the American Dream can reinforce the belief that more is always better. These influences can shape our habits, so understanding them is an essential step toward consistently making healthier financial choices.

The Freedom Seeker

The *freedom seeker* is a type of frugarian who adopts a frugal lifestyle because they're seeking independence from modern consumerism. They no longer want to be bound by debt, by high-stress/high-paying jobs, or by the expectations and perceptions of others. Freedom seekers aren't just people looking to retire early—they're often regular folks simply looking to downshift. Instead of working 60-hour weeks in high-stress jobs, they want to work part-time in roles with an easier pace or workload. Instead of killing themselves for $125K per year, they want to scale down to fewer weekly work hours in a lower-level position that pays for their needs, is enough for some of their wants, and leaves enough for modest savings and charity.

Freedom seekers understand that, in order to achieve a certain level of independence later, they have to make certain sacrifices now. If they want to stop working at age 60 or switch to part-time once they reach 50, there are steps they need to take to achieve those goals. Proper planning will not only help them save money but also prepare them for a future lifestyle without the burdens of debt. Instead of a retirement filled with high-priced "things" and expensive trips or excursions, they plan for a smaller or modified version to allow for greater financial freedom sooner.

I once had an acquaintance who was nearing the early-retirement age at her job. She worked hard to get out of debt and had adopted some frugal habits. She set aside a nest egg and had a plan to retire with her husband at age 55. What happened next is a classic example of people who get sucked in by the expectations of others. As the date drew near, the couple began to buy things to prepare for what they thought was going to be a fun, adventurous retirement. They splurged and bought many of their wants, regardless of whether they were actually needed. Their spending went unheeded for nearly six months before her retirement. As the bills started to become due, she quickly realized that the nest egg she had set aside was mostly spent, and she would need to continue working an additional five years—all because she wanted a sporty convertible like other retired couples, wanted to go to Palm Springs and other destinations like other retirees, and wanted to show off her "wealth" to her retired circle of friends.

In a similar situation, a freedom seeker would plan their retirement through the lens of frugality. They would assess whether the vehicle they have meets their needs instead of considering an additional car "just for fun". If they wanted a convertible to jaunt around the countryside, they may consider the cost of renting a ragtop sports car for a few days each summer instead of buying a second vehicle outright. A freedom seeker would strive to become *more* frugal in their retirement, not less. They would understand that the more consistent they are in their frugality, the longer they will be able to maintain their quality of life well into their golden years.

Goals

Whatever your goals are, it's important to keep them in mind as you embark on this journey—and to use them to refocus when you find yourself questioning whether this lifestyle is worth it. My frugal goals have changed many times throughout my life, and yours will, too. As we grow older, we gain wisdom and our perspectives shift. Sure, I still live with the frugality of a college student, but my goal now isn't to save on tuition or to rent an apartment within walking distance of campus. It's to prepare myself for forced early retirement due to chronic illness, to be able to earn my living in creative ways, and to earn back time that I can spend with my husband (hereafter "Hubby"), living in the most self-sustainable way we can.

The following are examples of common goals of frugarians. You don't have to embrace each one of these goals (or you may have some of your own), but they provide a good baseline to consider what you hope to accomplish by adopting a frugal lifestyle:

- To afford to live
- To save money
- To be debt-free
- To be less materialistic
- To be self-sufficient
- To hedge against economic instability and inflation
- To work less or downshift to a less stressful job
- To increase charitable giving
- To live more sustainably
- To leave a smaller environmental footprint

Affordable Living

At its most basic, the goal of frugality is survival. It's about ensuring that, no matter your circumstances or income, you have the means necessary to fulfill your fundamental needs. I provide more detail about assessing your basic needs later in this section.

Saving Money

One of the most common goals for people who adopt a frugal lifestyle is to save money. Having savings provides a sense of preparedness in the event of an emergency and offers the financial means for long-term planning. A nest egg helps ensure that the basic needs of your family will be covered for an extended period of time. Savings goals could range from squirrelling away a few hundred dollars for a new set of tires, to stocking your six-month emergency fund or a full retirement package to age 90. Individual reasons for saving money may differ, but the methods to accomplish those goals are often more easily achieved through a frugal lifestyle.

As a frugarian, saving money means consistently taking a percentage of your surplus budget and setting it aside for later. Your income could come from your regular 9-to-5 job, a side hustle, or something unexpected, like an inheritance or gift. The portion you choose to save is entirely up to you. Now, you may be reading this and thinking that your income currently barely covers your expenses. That may even be your motivation for adopting a frugal lifestyle. But as you make incremental changes, you should find that you're able to cover more of your basic needs—and may even have surplus funds to spare.

Being Debt-Free

Being debt-free is one of the most rewarding side effects of leading a frugal lifestyle. Once your debts are paid off, you'll have more financial freedom to set aside surplus funds for saving, investing, or other financial goals. At its core, debt is a form of financial slavery. With ever-increasing interest rates and transaction fees, the amount owed on credit cards and other high-interest loans can trap many people in a cycle they struggle to escape from. Another predatory financial trap is the vicious circle of payday loans: a borrower takes out $100, but with interest and fees, the repayment amount is $125. That $25 shortfall may force them to borrow again the following week, perpetuating the cycle.

Breaking free from debt can be very challenging, but it's a goal every frugarian should strive for. Even if you carry a debt load, such as a mortgage or student loan, your aim should be to pay it off as efficiently and quickly as possible.

Less Materialism

We are indeed living in a material world, but that doesn't mean we have to buy into it. Being constantly bombarded by media and marketing can make commercial items hard to resist. Even something as routine as driving around town can be tempting—with billboards, sales, and pushy retailers telling you exactly what you "can't live without".

The concept of ownership is a curious one in our modern age, particularly since the majority of purchases in North America are made with credit, not cash (1). We're constantly pressured by advertisements and the influence of others. We're told what we need, why we need it, what we'll gain by having it, and what we'll lose if we don't buy it. We fill our homes with things we believe reflect our success. We put on display how trendy we are, how well-travelled we are, how much we read, how great of an interior decorator we are, and so on—but for whose benefit?

When I think of the term "materialism", I'm immediately flung to the 1980s—a time of wealth and gaudy excess (think Elizabeth Taylor during the *Lifestyles of the Rich and Famous* era). Everything was bigger, louder, flashier, and more expensive. Status was defined by what people had, and the sentiment around purchases was often "the bigger, the better". The hairstyles and fashions may have changed, but the craving for more, more, more is stronger than ever—and many people have the bills and debt to prove it.

Frugarians see the underlying or alternative value in things and strive to surround themselves primarily with items that truly enrich their lives. The frugal lifestyle is rooted in the sentimental and the useful, rather than the purely material. The focus isn't on the cost of an item, but on your relationship to it. Perhaps it's a beautiful French landscape painting created by your grandfather during the war—it holds far more personal value than an expensive Thomas Kinkade lithograph purchased solely because it matched your décor.

Self-sufficiency

As you shake off the expectations of our modern world, you'll begin to discover the strength and power that comes from being able to provide for your family without being indebted to others. As you progress on your frugal journey, you'll grow your savings, learn to make do with what you have, and perhaps even resurrect skills that may have skipped a generation or two—such as crocheting your own throw blanket or giving your child's bicycle a tune-up.

The frugal lifestyle allows you to work towards self-sufficiency at your own pace. Maybe you'll start by honing your home cooking skills and getting creative with inexpensive pantry staples. As you progress, you may find yourself evolving into more of a homesteader-frugarian by starting a garden, raising a few chickens, or canning your surplus tomato harvest to last through spring. You may even begin exploring alternate forms of energy, such as a home wind turbine or a few small solar panels. By reducing your dependency on credit and moving away from the allure of material goods, you also free yourself from the burden of earning money to acquire them.

Economic Stability

Being frugal also helps buffer you from the economic instability caused by inflation, recession, and market volatility. During the Great Depression, my great-grandparents were just starting their young family. They had learned from their own parents about the hardships that came with WWI, such as rationing food and sundry items, or seeing homemakers transition into the workforce—it was a time of sacrifice and ingenuity. In hindsight, many who weathered the storm were frugarians who understood (even before the economic troubles hit) that living within your means, saving for a rainy day, and "making do or doing without" were essential.

Many people I've known from my grandparents' generation were able to adjust their standard of living during lean times by consistently being frugal and preparing for unforeseen events in times of plenty. The benefits of saving money for emergencies, building a pantry stockpile, and learning to enjoy life's simple pleasures will help you withstand even the most difficult situations, such as a job loss, an economic crash, a medical emergency, or a major weather event.

Living a simple, frugal life can also help you hedge against inflation. Staple food products like oats, rice, barley, carrots, cabbage, beets, beans, and potatoes have remained relatively affordable for the last 100 years. By building your family menus around basic, humble, and nourishing foods, you can avoid the unhealthy, highly processed versions —which often come in shrinking packages with ever-higher prices. As you fully immerse yourself in the frugal lifestyle, these types of preparations will become second nature and help you better prepare for economic circumstances that may negatively impact you and your family.

Work Less

Let's be honest: everyone would like to work less, especially with today's fast-paced corporate culture of unrealistic expectations and endless stress—and the relentless grind of being a cog in the so-called machine (which, incidentally, is largely fuelled by consumerism). By adopting a frugal lifestyle, many people find they have less need for high-stress/high-paying careers, because being a frugarian naturally reduces the demands on their bank account and eases the pressure to maintain those salaries.

In grade school, many of us were asked what we wanted to be when we grew up. We were asked about our goals and what our adulthood would be like (I distinctly remember forecasting my future in the year 2000—flying cars and all). At that age, we based our career choices on simple factors, like whether we'd get to play with animals or drive with the sirens on. By junior high, we were expected to tailor our futures to fit our interests, talents, and life goals. We were told that the only path to success was to go to college, spend a fortune on a degree, and land a well-paying job. Everyone needed a fancy career with plenty of disposable income to build a happy family and to afford a nice home with a garage full of toys. We later rationalized the stress, long hours, and time away from our families as "livin' the dream".

It's common for new adopters of a frugal lifestyle to scale back once they've reached certain financial goals or milestones. It's not unusual to see frugarians in high-level corporate positions downshift to lower-stress, lower-paying roles. Others continue in the same job but set firm boundaries around the hours they're willing to work. Another popular option is moving from full-time to part-time hours—something frugarians can do more easily because the extra income isn't needed to pay off debt or stockpile more "status stuff".

In my experience, I worked my way up to a senior analyst role in a local government office. I had opportunities to advance further, but when I looked at my friends and colleagues in those high-level positions, it seemed like more stress than it was worth. I currently have minimal work stress, modest levels of responsibility, and enough salary to live a comfortable, yet frugal, lifestyle. Ultimately, I would like to continue downshifting, and likely will as I get older. Early retirement is a motivator, but I also like the idea of earning a living through writing and freelance editing—still working, but working differently, less often, and for myself. This circles back to the concept of embracing frugality as a means of self-sufficiency.

Charitable Giving

One of the most worthwhile goals of those living a frugal lifestyle is the ability to increase charitable giving. There is comfort in knowing that your basic needs are met to the extent that you can share some of your surplus with others in need. Charity doesn't have to be monetary, either. You may find that your frugal lifestyle frees up more of your time to offer meaningful gestures, like volunteering at a food bank, helping deliver meals to the elderly, or pulling weeds in your community garden. Your charity can also take the form of sharing your frugal skills with others. Are you good at canning? Does your elderly neighbour have a giant apple tree but isn't sure how to process all the fruit? Lending your skills to someone in need is a wonderful way to frugally share the gift of charity.

Apprehensions

Adopting a frugal lifestyle isn't a decision to take lightly. It requires a great deal of commitment, ingenuity, and thick skin. For some, frugality can be drastically different from the way they currently live and spend. Many people avoid adopting a frugal lifestyle simply because spending money on whatever they want feels easier—until the bills arrive, until they're working overtime to pay them off, and until they realize they're missing out on time and experiences with their loved ones.

Common "frugal fears" include:

- Fear of missing out
- Fear of doing without
- Fear of change
- Fear of failure
- Worrying about what others think

Fear of Missing Out

The fear of missing out (FOMO) can be a huge barrier for people exploring the frugal lifestyle. There's a stereotype that frugarians don't do anything fun because everything fun costs money, but I've found the opposite to be true. Many frugarians get to experience *more* because the focus is on the uniqueness of the experience and the people they're spending time with—not on how much money was spent.

When I consider an activity, like going out for dinner and drinks, I think about what I'm trying to accomplish—time with friends, tasty food, a cool environment, and a couple of hours away from the house. When you strip an activity down to its base goals, the location (such as a trendy lounge with $15 cocktails) often doesn't matter, because you're still meeting several of those goals. For example, when you invite a group of friends over for board games, you can ask them to bring their favourite treats to add to your snack spread, along with their own (alcoholic) beverages. That way, you're still spending time with them, trying new foods, and unwinding—all while keeping your costs to a minimum. You may even find that the conversation and interactions at home are far better than at a restaurant or bar—you're able to talk, the lighting is normal, and you're not competing with the DJ and their loud (and often terrible) music.

To change things up, try rotating whose house each get-together is held at. You can also play around with locations depending on the season. In the summer, you could spend a day doing field activities with a picnic in a nearby park. In the winter, swap board games for ice skates and head down to a community rink with a thermos of homemade hot chocolate. This approach works for nearly any activity you can think of. Want to go to a movie? Borrow a DVD from the public library, pop some popcorn, and invite friends over to watch. Want to go shopping with your girlfriends? Arrange a clothing swap where everyone brings clothes to exchange, along with a funny story about where they bought or wore them. Consider the creativity required to plan activities with minimal resources—you can even engage your children and friends to make the prep work and anticipation part of the fun.

By letting go of the expectation to be involved in everything all the time (even activities you don't particularly enjoy), you'll begin to see how your frugal lifestyle is positively impacting your relationships. You'll move away from the FOMO mentality and the lifestyle perpetuated by unrealistic posts and ads on social media. Over time, you'll start to recognize that you're creating your own special memories and fostering deeper, more meaningful connections with your family and friends.

Doing Without

In a similar vein as FOMO is the fear of doing without. Humans are creatures of habit and comfort—most of us strive to create environments for work, play, and rest that are routine, stable, and enjoyable. Frugality isn't about doing without (necessarily), but about clearly identifying your needs while making room for select wants. It's about making do *with*. Once you understand your needs and what you can't live without, you'll be better able to see that everything else is a bonus.

"Doing without" essentially means not consuming something—either because you can't afford it or because you don't want to spend the money on it. "Doing with" means allowing yourself the freedom to make a purchase, but doing so through the lens of frugality. It's seeing if there's a way to use what you already have to meet that need. It's looking for the item at a thrift store, finding opportunities to trade or barter, or seeing if you can get it on clearance. Most importantly, it's ensuring that you're not going into debt to buy it.

Hubby works from home, and due to the unusual hours of his job (and the fact that his office is the living room), it's essential that I have my own space to watch movies, write, read, or just unwind. I created a space for myself in our teeny little spare room—it has a closing door, light, power, and a window. When I set out to furnish the room, I knew I didn't want to spend much money, so I set a budget of $500. I needed a TV, a table for the TV, a comfortable recliner, some bookshelves, lighting, and a few art pieces or wall hangings to spice it up a bit.

I did what a lot of my friends do—I created a Pinterest board. It helped me come up with ideas for how to organize and furnish the small room to make it feel larger. Instead of heading to Amazon or Wayfair, though, I shopped our garage, basement, other rooms, and closets. I snagged the bookshelves from the garage that Hubby and I had stored when we moved in together. I rummaged through the spare room and grabbed the small TV that wasn't really being used. Then I dug through our electronics junk drawer and found an old pair of desktop speakers to give the TV better audio.

My next step was to make a list of what I still needed: a table for the TV, an area rug, a lamp, and some artwork. I found a giant oil painting print of macro poppies for $20 at Goodwill—it's huge and gives the room a big splash of orange and red. I also bought a small area rug and lamp for half price at Winners. I scored a discounted La-Z-Boy from their clearance outlet for $300. The whole room ended up complete, cute, and totally functional for a grand total of about $450—affordable and under budget. In the process, I had fun redecorating my little she-cave and didn't go without anything, other than a giant amount owing on my credit card.

Worrying About What Others Think

It's probably not surprising that most people's number one concern in life is themselves. That's not to say they don't care about others—it just means that instead of worrying about what you're wearing, how you look, where you live, what you drive, or the latest vacation you took, they're more focused on what *they're* wearing, how *they* look, where *they* live, what *they* drive, and what you think about *their* latest vacation. When most people "dress to impress", they're doing just that—looking for validation from others that their choice of outfit was a good one. If most people are preoccupied with how they're being perceived, it's likely they're not paying much mind to others.

I mention this because of the famous notion of "Keeping up with the Joneses". There's a lot of pride and self-adulation that comes with going into debt to make it appear as if you're more successful or privileged than you are. That may feel harsh to read, but it makes me wonder: why does society have such an ingrained need to show off our successes to others? I believe that it's rooted, once again, in the concept of the American Dream and decades of highly effective, targeted advertising.

For many newly frugal people, it's a huge relief to realize that their consumerism doesn't need to be dictated by the expectations of others. No one in your mommy group cares if your baby stroller was a hand-me-down from your sister instead of a boutique brand with a $1,000 price tag. No one at your college cares if you bought your like-new backpack and school binders from a thrift store instead of the campus bookstore. No one cares if you wear the same little black dress to the work Christmas party each year. No one cares if you got your winter tires from some guy on Kijiji instead of a dealership.

If you're a woman, consider what you wear day-to-day, how you style your hair, and the details of how you apply your makeup. Most people are so preoccupied with how they look that they're rarely inclined to notice whether or not you have the latest designer handbag, wear expensive clothes, or get $200 haircuts. Likewise, they wouldn't notice that your cute purse was $3 from the flea market, that you transitioned to a natural, makeup-free look years ago, or that you trim the ends of your hair with a thrifted pair of salon shears that you sharpen yourself.

If you're a man, the same considerations apply. The guys at the office wouldn't notice that your vintage silk tie was $6 from Savers or that your most recent haircut was done by a student at the barber college. No one would bat an eye if you showed up to your worksite with a pair of second-hand coveralls or a like-new hard hat you purchased from eBay.

Letting go of the expectations of others is a great relief—it frees your mind to focus on other things while also freeing up the dollars in your pocketbook. When you're no longer trapped in the "consume and compare" cycle, there's less compulsion to buy the latest and greatest (and most expensive) when serviceable, humble, and modest will do just as well.

Fear of Change

Humans are habitual. Most of us don't thrive on change, and we like our patterns and routines. We tend to avoid major disruptions to the way we do things—or respond poorly when we have no other choice. Transitioning to a frugal lifestyle is a big change, but it doesn't have to be intimidating, difficult, or overwhelming. It can be an exciting, fun, and rewarding experience.

One of the easiest ways to adapt to change is to move at your own pace. For some, that may mean an overnight, cold-turkey switch to frugality. For others, it will be a more gradual transition—starting with a few minor changes and evolving into more fluid and frequent behaviours. Small changes could include creating your week's meal plan based on sale-priced items in the grocery store flyer. It could also mean doing a sweep of the fridge and freezer for any old or slightly freezer-burnt items you already have on hand, making sure nothing goes to waste.

It doesn't have to be a drastic change to be meaningful.

You can make the transition to frugality fun by setting yourself small goals and challenges. One of the first lifestyle tweaks I recommend is to set a goal of cutting your grocery bill in half for one week. So, if you normally spend $200 per week for a family of four, see what you can do on a budget of $100. Most people, with a little bit of ingenuity and a dash of sacrifice, can make that $100 goal—all while enjoying the process of creating new recipes, cooking new foods, and eating hearty home-cooked meals.

A frugal habit I adopted during college was using meat alternatives. I was on a limited budget and couldn't afford to purchase meat for more than one meal per day. I looked for budget options, like using roasted peanuts in a stir-fry instead of chicken breast, or making pasta with beans instead of spaghetti with sausage and beef meatballs (check out *Laura in the Kitchen* on YouTube for her delectable Pasta e Fagioli recipe). I still made room for some of my favourite dishes, but I gradually began adding more and more frugal menu items to my repertoire—and now I find that my frugal recipes are among my favourites.

Fear of Failure

The fear of failure is also a stumbling block for some people considering the frugal lifestyle. There's a perception that frugality is a rigid set of rules and steps you must follow—and if you don't do it "correctly", other frugarians will notice and call you out on it.

Frugality is literally foolproof. There is no way to do it wrong, mess up, or fail while trying to adopt frugal habits. Even if you technically fail at a task, you're still learning—and no opportunity to learn can be considered a failure. Frugality is all about trying new things, thinking outside the box, and approaching each new endeavour with a bag full of learned experiences.

Part 2
Understanding Wants and Needs

When was the last time you really needed something? Maybe you told yourself you needed a new pumpkin-spice-coloured sweater because summer was transitioning into fall. Maybe you needed to stop at the coffee shop on the way to pick up your best friend because you needed a double-shot caramel macchiato. The concept of "need" has been corrupted by the human compulsion to see everything we want *really badly* as something we need to survive.

Our Basic Needs
A "need" is something you require because it's essential or very important (2). Think about the basic things that everyone needs in order to survive in our modern world. The basic needs for humans are:

- Food and water
- Shelter
- Transportation
- Clothing
- Utilities and communication
- Social contact and love
- Education

Food and Water
Obviously, humans can't live without food and water. They're the most fundamental of our basic needs—and for good reason. You need food

for nourishment, sustenance, vitamins, minerals, and the fuel to supply your body and mind with energy. You need water to keep your cells and organs hydrated, and to maintain healthy skin, nails, and hair. In addition to the chemical and biological needs of our bodies, food is also a conduit for another of our basic needs: social interaction. Food is the fruit of love, and so many of our relationships, memories, and experiences are fostered around shared meals.

When you think about your food needs, focus on the nutrients and minerals required to sustain human life. Consider the number of daily calories everyone in your family needs to maintain an active, healthy body weight. Reflect on any special dietary or health needs, as well as any special circumstances in your daily life—such as the need to pack a lunch for work or to budget money for your child's school lunch program. You should also think about whether you have reliable access to clean water and a means to store it for emergencies. Finally, take a moment to consider whether you use food for nourishment—or for comfort and entertainment.

Basic Needs for Food and Water

- Enough healthy and nourishing food to meet the dietary requirements of an active, healthy lifestyle for each member of your household
- A means to store your food and protect it from spoilage
- Consideration for allergy and dietary requirements
- Packed lunches for school and/or office
- Packed meals or dining out for work and/or business travel
- Clean, potable tap water
- Storage containers for water
- Water filters and/or water purification tablets

Shelter

When you consider your basic needs for shelter, it's important to include everyone in your household. For some, shelter needs may be a studio apartment—others may require a full mother-in-law suite with several bedrooms, depending on how many people are living there. Every room in your home should have a specific purpose, but the individual needs of each family member will vary based on their interests, hobbies, and activities.

As you move through the "Minimize and Organize" section later in the book, you'll examine your specific needs in each room of your house. As you progress through those exercises, you may discover that you have much more house than you actually need, that your space is too small to provide your family with comfortable shelter—or that the amount of room in your home is just right. If your home is much larger than required, it may be time to consider a minimalist approach and downsize to a smaller space. If it's too small, frugal living is an ideal way to cut costs and save towards a goal of a larger home.

Basic Needs for Shelter:

- A self-contained space that protects from natural and physical elements (weather, animal predators, intruders, insects, etc.)
- Utilities and plumbing
- Sleeping and resting areas
- Meal preparation and food storage areas and equipment
- Washrooms and shower facilities
- Laundry facilities

Transportation

Transportation is all about how you get from one place to another. When selecting my current residence and neighbourhood, I was mindful to choose a location with easy access to public transit, so I could reduce spending by not using a car for my daily commute. My monthly transportation expenses are around $100 for an unlimited bus pass. Hubby has a car, but he works from home, so we really only use it on weekends for running errands and buying groceries.

Take a moment to think about how you currently get around your city or town. Do you drive everywhere? Does your household have more than one vehicle? Is there a bus route near your home? Do you have a bicycle and helmet collecting dust in your garage?

Your transportation needs will vary based on your job, your family's specific daily routines, and what you can afford. If you have a job on the other side of the city and taking the bus would eat up several hours of commute time every day, it makes sense for you to have a car. If you live within a short distance of your workplace and could take the bus or walk, you may not need a car at all. I know several frugarians who take a taxi home from the grocery store once or twice per month instead of paying for gas, insurance, and registration for a car they rarely drive.

When considering your transportation needs, think about the size of your family and the age of everyone who would be riding in the vehicle. For instance, if it's just you and your spouse, there would be little need for a deluxe minivan—but if you have a large family with children under the age of three, it wouldn't make sense for your only vehicle to be a fancy 2-seater sports car. If you have more than one vehicle, it may be an opportunity to downsize.

Basic Needs for Transportation
- Walking shoes
- Bicycle
- Bus pass or commuter rail pass
- Reliable vehicle
- Airfare and/or taxi fares for business travel
- Considerations for different times of the year (winter tires, etc.)

Clothing and Shoes

Clothing is one of our primary needs because it helps us stay warm and protected. The clothing needs for each member of your household will differ based on their sex, age, occupation, and activities. For example, you may work with heavy machinery and need a pair of safety gloves and a hard hat. Maybe you work in a professional kitchen and need whites and chef's pants. Perhaps you work in an executive office where you're required to follow a strict business attire dress code.

Consider the clothing needs of your family:

- Does everyone in your household have the items they need to stay covered and warm in every season?
- Does anyone in your household need clothing for a specific job or activity?

Basic Needs for Clothing and Shoes

- Clothing and shoes to keep you and your family warm in every season for your climate/region
- Clothing and shoes required for specific jobs or activities (for example, steel-toed boots because you work on construction sites)
- Clothing and shoes required to meet workplace or school dress code requirements

Utilities and Communication

Utilities are often overlooked as one of our fundamental needs. Food is crucial, but you need electricity, gas, or firewood to cook it. Shelter is mandatory, but you need gas to heat the furnace and hot water tank, and electricity for lights and appliances. Washrooms are vital, but you need water and sewage facilities to keep things moving.

In our modern age, access to the internet is essential. For even our most basic activities—like school, banking, and telecommuting—the internet is the utility that connects us to the rest of the world. As an undergraduate (2000 to 2006), I couldn't afford a computer or internet of my own, so I took advantage of the free resources at the university and public libraries. I was able to save my work to a portable USB drive and use their printers for a small fee. Once I secured a job in my field after college, I was able to get in-home internet and a laptop—but I still opted for a modest computer model and the least expensive internet plan to stay within my budget.

Being able to communicate with others over the phone is also a necessity. Whether it's to connect with friends and family, book appointments, or speak with customer service, most people use the phone frequently in their daily lives. Smartphones have been popular since the early 2010s, and for some of us, they're an essential tool. However, it's important to remember that many features fall into the "want" category: music, apps, games, and additional data.

Consider what type of device and service plan you need for your day-to-day communication. Your school-aged children may only need a simple pay-as-you-go flip phone with no data if it's just a way to stay in touch when they're away from home. Your spouse may need a smartphone with the latest features and the largest data plan because of work, business, or travel commitments. You may find that you don't use the phone much at all and only need a landline (yes, they still exist!) with local calling and pay-per-minute long distance.

While your device and plan selections will be based on your individual needs, it's important to consider the element of distraction that comes from regularly using smartphones. There's a growing movement in frugal circles where people are replacing their smartphones with "dumb phones"—phones without internet access and with pay-per-call/text plans. By moving away from smartphones for entertainment and returning to basic phones for communication, you'll model a frugal lifestyle while freeing up time to engage with others in real life rather than online (and save money to boot).

Basic Needs for Utilities and Communication
- Heat
- Water
- Electricity
- Waste disposal and sewage
- Internet access
- Telephone and service plan

Social Contact and Love
When people consider their basic needs, their minds often go straight to consumable goods and material stuff they can stuff their homes with. Often forgotten are the most basic of human needs: social interaction and love. Regardless of social class, location, race, gender, or ethnicity— we all have the innate need for intimate relationships. As frugarians, it's a bonus that this is also the least expensive of our essentials. It costs nothing to be kind, to show love and affection, to be a friend in need, or to meet up with others for an engaging conversation. You don't have to pull out your wallet to hug a friend, and you don't have to dip into your savings to give your grandpa a phone call.

The base motivation of frugality is to lead a fulfilling life in which you spend time and share experiences with others. By participating in activities, education, meals, and other events as a group, you'll create memories while naturally fostering intimacy and connection. Social contact and love are also correlated with charitable giving. Shared experiences can be initiated through kindness and generosity of spirit toward everyone—not just friends and family.

Basic Needs for Social Contact and Love

- Close personal relationships with family and friends
- Close relationships within your personal faith community
- Interaction within your local community
- Shared experiences
- Physical contact
- Recognition of body language and facial expressions

Education

One of my favourite movie lines ever is from a classic scene in *Good Will Hunting*. Will confronts a bully in a Harvard bar about his pretension and lack of originality: "You dropped 150 grand on an education you could have got for $1.50 in late charges at the public library".

It always strikes me as funny because the statement is absolutely true—it costs nothing to educate yourself. Sure, you may not get a Harvard degree for free, but any topic you want to learn about should be accessible to you in the information age. Whether you find free courses on sites like LinkedIn Learning, edX, or Coursera, you have the ability to learn valuable skills for very little money.

College is beneficial in many ways, but corporate recruiters often prefer practical experience to education. It's a common misconception that it's impossible to get a foot in the door without a degree—but with the popularity and recognition of Massive Open Online Courses (MOOCs) offered by prominent educational institutions, it's possible to complete coursework online for free that you can then apply in real-world settings.

Hubby is an example of someone who paid little to nothing for his education and now has a well-paying job. Sure, he took coursework throughout his 25 years in the field, but he was rarely the one who paid for it—the cost was usually part of corporate training, covered as a performance incentive, or something he completed on his own through various free MOOCs. Not only that, but since his work in IT is constantly evolving, he's able to maintain his knowledge base through free online articles, forums, and webinars.

My educational experience is on the other end of the spectrum. I have multiple degrees, all of which I paid for through student loans, grants, bursaries, scholarships, and part-time work while I was in school. While practical experience in my field (records and information management) is essential, there are limited opportunities to gain that experience without formal tuition.

Before deciding which educational path to take, consider exploring trades or careers best suited to on-the-job learning. Some professions offer a stepped approach, such as apprenticeships, to gain higher certifications and accreditation. As a new frugarian, research the average salary for careers at different stages after graduation (e.g., 1 to 5 years, 5 to 10 years)—for some jobs, you may not earn a livable wage for several years. This delay can be mitigated by choosing a field with an integrated apprenticeship program or by completing unpaid internships during your degree to gain hands-on experience before graduating. Whether you're at the start of your career, seeking a change, or guiding your teenage children as they come of age, viewing education through the lens of frugality can not only save money but also prepare you for the realities of working to live, rather than living to work.

Basic Needs for Education
- Standard K–12 public education or access to homeschooling materials
- Access to information resources, such as the public library
- Internet access
- Willing and supportive family and friends who will foster curiosity with opportunities for learning and mentorship

Our Deepest Wants

"Wants" are the things we desire but don't need to meet our basic requirements for survival. They offer short-term gratification, often serve a limited purpose, and frequently cost more than their long-term value justifies. But being frugal doesn't mean eliminating the things you want—it means taking the time to assess whether an item will genuinely bring lasting joy and fulfillment to your life.

Keeping up with the Joneses

In a former job of mine, I worked with various senior executives and high-level stakeholders. Due to the nature of the business, we were required to dress in business casual attire at the office. I could have gone to Dillard's or Holt Renfrew to buy designer outfits at $1,000 a pop— but as a frugarian, I took a different approach.

Several years ago, I decided to adopt a simple, classic style. Since I wasn't (and still am not) persuaded by trends or designer brands, I frequented thrift stores, consignment shops, and garage sales, and scoured the online clearance sections of my favourite retailers. I still looked polished and business-appropriate without worrying about wearing the latest designer fashions.

Hubby took a similar approach as he moved up the corporate ladder. Because he was interacting with clients outside of work and visiting job sites as a representative of his employer, he understood the importance of projecting success—so he needed a vehicle that aligned with that image. Did he go out and buy a brand-new Land Rover? BMW? Audi? No, he bought a 10-year-old Ford Explorer. It was a fraction of the price of a high-end luxury car, was in great condition, and didn't look out of place in the parking lot with its classic gunmetal grey and chrome trim. It had low mileage, and the previous owner had kept it pristine. Do you think anyone noticed he wasn't driving a fancy luxury car? No! While his coworkers were working long hours and complaining about the high interest and monthly payments on their vehicles, he bought a car he could afford (and paid cash) because he wasn't worried about "Keeping up with the Joneses".

Envy of what other people have (or what we *perceive* they have) can have devastating impacts on more than just our wallets. Our self-esteem can suffer because, in our constant quest to keep up, we never stop to take stock and be grateful for what we *do* have—we just focus on what's missing (whether we actually need it or not). Being grateful for the things you already have makes you more appreciative. A side benefit is that you tend to take better care of those things, because you're more conscious of the real value they provide.

Desire is tough to resist because we're constantly tempted. Whether it's a result of being advertised to or simply the human drive to show our success, desire is one of the biggest obstacles for people entering the frugal lifestyle. For most of us, it takes a great deal of discipline to consistently practice frugality. It's not because the lifestyle itself is hard—it's because we are constantly coaxed and cajoled to consume. From the moment we leave our house, the consumption train starts. Turn on the car, burn fuel. Drive by McDonald's, buy a McMuffin. Park near the corner store, grab a magazine that shows you everything else you need to consume. By turning off the "Keeping up with the Joneses" switch, you're freeing yourself from the endless temptation to buy, buy, buy.

Pride is another motivator for people striving to keep up with the Joneses. Pride of ownership. Pride from compliments. Pride in knowing how much you spent on an item and pride in the expectation of receiving praise for having it. Frugarians aren't immune to prideful thoughts, but those thoughts often take a very different perspective. Perhaps it's the pride of accomplishment in paying down a mortgage in half the time, or in getting a compliment on a blouse you found in the rummage bin at the thrift store. It could be taking pride in knowing that the basic needs of your family are consistently met.

Before making a purchase, ask yourself if you're trying to keep up with the Joneses. Dig deep into why you feel the need to do so, and whether you honestly care what others think. You may be surprised by your answers—you may be spending out of obligation to a fantasy of success rather than out of actual need.

Satisfying Wants

Adopting a frugal lifestyle doesn't mean you have to focus solely on needs or that you can't occasionally purchase items you want. Frugality is more about finding joy in simply meeting your needs while satisfying your wants with things that bring lasting enjoyment and value. An example from our family is when we saved to buy a larger entertainment system—something we would consider pretty fancy. Hubby had bought high-quality speakers second-hand about 15 years earlier, so all we needed was an upgraded TV. Knowing we would be spending a lot of time at home with friends and family, we decided to make the investment. We waited for Boxing Day sales and saved on a slightly older model of our preferred screen. Not only did we improve our movie-watching experience, but we also now enjoy spending more time with each other and with the people we love. As an added frugal benefit, we're saving money by not going to movie theatres to spend $20 each on tickets, plus another $50 on beverages and snacks.

A big part of the frugal lifestyle is striving to be debt-free and resisting the urge to buy things you can't afford. When we bought our new TV, we saved up for it and waited until it was on sale. It took a little longer for us to get what we wanted, but that made the purchase more worthwhile—we saw it as a reward for hard work and sacrifice. The first night we sat down to a library-rented movie with our homemade popcorn, there was no burden of debt on our minds because it was paid for in full. As you become more comfortable with the frugal lifestyle, this way of thinking will become second nature. You'll become far more discerning about the cost-to-value ratio of each purchase and the effort required to earn the money to pay for it.

Peer Pressure

One of the challenges new frugarians sometimes face is peer pressure—feeling obligated to do something you don't really want to do because others are pressuring you. People succumb to peer pressure for a variety of reasons, from wanting to be "in" or popular to wanting to avoid potential conflicts. I understand it can be difficult (I'm a classic people-pleaser), but you can develop the ability to say "no" to situations that go against your new frugal lifestyle. A simple strategy is to be open and upfront with your friends and family about what you're doing. Communicate your frugal goals and how much you would appreciate their support. A light word of caution: your lifestyle shift may cause rifts or a distancing of superficial friendships.

As you grow more comfortable with your frugality, opportunities may arise for you to suggest frugal options for workplace activities and events. In my office, colleagues have vastly different salary ranges—from the mailroom to the boardroom. Because of this diversity, many activities, such as expensive lunches out or trips to the movie theatre or bowling alley, are proportionally more costly for team members with lower incomes. We addressed that disparity by focusing on activities that didn't cost much (or any) money. Instead of an expensive lunch out during the holiday season, we would have a festive potluck where everyone brought their favourite dish to share. On one occasion, a colleague thanked me for suggesting a potluck dinner for our summer staff party because it was an event she could actually afford—she could enjoy the festivities without worrying throughout dinner about how much the bill would be at the end.

Part 3
The Sweep

The Sweep is the next step in transitioning to a frugal lifestyle. It's essentially a current-state assessment of your life and spending habits, and an opportunity to consider and evaluate the true basic needs of you and your family. The Sweep is a chance to get organized and set out a plan for your frugal life going forward. The past experiences and motivations of each frugarian are different, and the time it takes to assess your life and behaviours is wholly personal. Take it easy on yourself. It won't happen overnight—and it doesn't have to. Every change you make is a positive step forward in your frugal journey.

As you go through each room in your house, you're not only taking stock of what you already have, but also looking for what's missing from your daily needs. It's an opportunity to identify other items in your home—often in the attic, basement, or garage—that could be used instead. It gives you a chance to see how much of your money is being spent on things that don't serve a long-term purpose or hold enduring personal meaning. The Sweep is also an exercise to help determine which items in your home could be useful later—such as saving your children's toys for future grandchildren. The Sweep is truly the start of minimizing your life and maximizing your frugal potential.

For this activity, I suggest using a small notebook to outline what you need to meet the basic needs of your family in each room of your home, as listed below. Start with the largest items, such as beds or tables, and work your way down to the smallest, such as desk lamps or wastepaper baskets. Keep in mind that each family member will have specific, individual needs.

Things to consider as you Sweep each room:

- What do you need to meet your basic needs for survival?
- What do you need to meet the basic needs of your family?
- Are there items in the room that you don't need?
- Could any of the things you don't need in that room fill a need elsewhere?
- Are any of the basic needs of you or your family missing?

The following are examples of rooms in many North American homes:

- Kitchen
- Bathroom
- Living room
- Dining room
- Master bedroom
- Children's bedroom(s)
- Laundry room
- Garage
- Basement
- Home office

As you move through your home and begin your assessment, you'll find that your needs vary depending on the room. The needs for a bathroom are very different from those for a kitchen or home office. Once you identify your needs, take a moment to jot them down in your notebook. Keep an eye out for those items at thrift stores, garage sales, swap meets, flea markets, online clearance sections, discount retailers—and especially in other rooms of your home.

Basic Kitchen Needs

A well-stocked kitchen is essential for a frugarian because one of the easiest ways to ease into the lifestyle and make lasting changes to your budget is to prepare most of your meals from scratch. Home cooking becomes much easier with the right equipment and tools. As with each subsequent room, the items listed below are examples only and should serve as a guide—not a strict list you must follow to be frugal.

Hubby and I started our couplehood in a one-room studio basement suite. The room was just big enough to hold a double bed, two chairs, and a TV—with a tiny kitchenette and bathroom attached. Our cookware collection began modestly, with one general pot, a frying pan, a cookie sheet, some cutlery, spatulas, and dishware. Over time, it grew to include most items on this needs list. In the last couple of years, we've also been able to purchase a few wants, like a stand mixer and a high-speed blender. We bought them new at a steep discount, and since we use them so often in our home cooking, they have enduring value.

We have also found some hidden gems for the kitchen at thrift stores. Some of our best finds include an 8" Henckels chef's knife for $4 and a 10" All-Clad stainless steel sauté pan for $5. We sometimes break water glasses or snack bowls, and always buy replacement dishes second-hand. The colour of our dishes is a light blue-grey, so we simply mix and match new pieces within the same colour palette.

The following are examples of basic items needed for a well-stocked kitchen:

Electrical and Lighting
- Overhead light
- Countertop electrical outlets

Appliances

- Fridge
- Stove
- Oven
- Coffee maker
- Tea kettle
- Toaster
- Kitchen scale

Furniture
- Kitchen table and chairs (one chair per family member)

Cooking Equipment
- Stockpot
- Dutch oven
- Cast-iron pan
- Small, medium, and large heavy-bottomed pots (opt for stainless steel if possible)
- Large non-stick frying pan
- Small non-stick frying pan
- Deep-sided frying pan or wok
- Non-stick baking trays (one large and one medium)
- Non-stick cake pans (one 8×8 in., one 9×11 in., and two round)
- Nesting glass or steel bowls
- Casserole dish (if you can get one with a lid, even better)
- Non-stick muffin tins (one 12-hole and one 6-hole)
- Loaf pans (two to four pans, depending on your family size)
- Immersion blender
- Hand mixer
- Large black enamel roasting pan with lid (pioneer-style)

- Colander
- Fine-mesh strainer
- Cutting boards
- Well-made, sharp kitchen knives (chef's knife, paring knife, utility knife, and serrated knife, at a minimum—it will make home cooking easier and more enjoyable, so they're well worth the investment)
- Two-sided wet sharpening stone

Utensils

- Cutlery (two per family member of forks, soup spoons, tea spoons, butter knives, and steak knives)
- Wooden spoons
- Slotted spoon
- Ladle
- Cooking spatulas (flippers)
- Baking spatulas
- Whisk
- Pastry cutter
- Bench scraper
- Measuring cups (for both liquid and dry ingredients)

Dishes

- Water glasses (two per family member)
- Coffee/tea cups (two per family member)
- Plates and bowls (two per family member of dinner plates, sandwich plates, and soup bowls)

<u>Storage and Waste</u>

- Pantry or cupboards for food storage
- Cupboards for dishes, cooking equipment, and storage containers
- Food storage containers (use glass when possible)
- Cupboard for cleaning supplies and a dirty towel bucket (under the sink is ideal)
- Trash can
- Recycling bin

<u>Linen</u>

- Kitchen hand towels (for drying clean hands only)
- Kitchen towels (for cooking and tidying up instead of paper towels)
- Oven mitts

<u>Health and Safety</u>

- Fire extinguisher
- First-aid kit

<u>Miscellaneous</u>

- Parchment paper
- Aluminum foil
- Cling film
- Muffin cups

Basic Bathroom Needs

The bathroom needs of each family vary, but at its most basic, a bathroom is simply a place to get clean and use the toilet. While we might all love a jacuzzi tub, his-and-her sinks, and a floor-length mirror, our actual needs are quite simple.

In our home, we have a tub with a shower attachment (and a water filter that we change every six months because of our city's extremely hard water), a shower curtain liner, and a decorative shower curtain—which we've had for the fifteen years we've been together, plus the five years that Hubby had it prior to that. We also have a sink with under-cabinets, a medicine cabinet, a mirror, overhead lighting, a bath mat, a towel rack, robe hooks, a trash can, a recycling basket, a toilet brush, a plunger, and a toilet paper holder. Under the sink, we keep our sponges, cleaning supplies, scrub brushes, and a stockpile of personal hygiene products.

We've had most of our bathroom linens for over ten years and only buy new items if they become stained or threadbare (which we then save for rags). Personally, I prefer a well-worn, thin towel, but Hubby likes them light and fluffy—so he gets first dibs on the new towels, and I use the older ones. Thrift stores are also a good option for towels. When I was just starting out, I got all of mine from Value Village and even managed to find a matching bath mat.

The following are examples of basic items needed in a practical and comfortable bathroom:

Electrical and Lighting
- Overhead light
- Bathroom-safe electrical outlet

Fixtures
- Toilet
- Sink with cabinet
- Shower
- Medicine cabinet
- Towel rack
- Mirror
- Toilet paper holder

<u>Storage and Waste</u>
- Trash can

<u>Linens</u>
- Bath towels, hand towels, and facecloths (two of each per family member)
- Shower curtain
- Bath mat

<u>Health and Safety</u>
- First-aid kit
- Medicines and vitamins
- Prescriptions
- Dental items
- Soaps, scents, and shampoos
- Shaving items

<u>Miscellaneous</u>
- Cleaning products, sponges, and scrub brushes
- Toilet brush
- Plunger

Basic Living Room Needs

Needs for a living room are based on several factors, including the size of your family and the types of activities they're involved in. Considering the activities that usually occur in your living room will help you determine how much space you need and what furniture best suits the space. If you don't have company very often, you may only need a couch for seating. However, if you're part of a book club that meets monthly at your place, you may need a couch, a loveseat, and a couple of side chairs.

The same can be said for deciding whether or not you need a television. Some frugal families prefer non-media forms of entertainment—reading, arts and crafts, or athletics. Others choose to have a TV but don't pay for cable—instead, they keep a stash of their favourite videos and borrow new-to-them titles from the library. Hubby and I like to hook into streaming services for a low monthly fee rather than shelling out the inflated rates for cable (and we always make sure to take advantage of free trials).

As you assess your living room furniture needs, be mindful of the quality and durability of the items—especially if you need to buy something new. As a frugarian, your focus should be on things that last rather than items that are cheap and trendy. I like new styles as much as the next person, but I can't justify spending money on something that's going to break down or wear out in a year or two. For example, if you get a couch with durable, stain-resistant upholstery, you won't have to pay later for cleaning or reupholstering. Stains will be minor, and you can handle them yourself without damaging the fabric.

Luckily, furniture is one of the best values at thrift stores and garage sales. You can often pick up quality pieces for a good price instead of opting for cheaper alternatives that are much lower quality. As part of our living room assessment, Hubby and I knew we needed a coffee table—but as frugarians, we also knew we didn't want to spend much. We wanted the table to be something we'd only need to buy once in our lifetime, if we could help it, so it had to be made of real wood. We ended up purchasing our coffee table for only $40 on Kijiji (an online platform similar to Facebook Marketplace). It's a beautiful hardwood with a cherry stain and matte finish. We chose this piece because it was durable and matched our other thrifted furniture. Be sure to check out your local buy-and-sell sites for second-hand staples for your living room.

The following are examples of basic items needed in a comfortable living room:

<u>Electrical and Lighting</u>
- Overhead light or lamps
- Internet and cable hook-ups
- Extension cords and power bars

<u>Furniture</u>
- Couch and other seating
- Coffee table
- End tables
- Curtains
- Carpet

<u>Storage and Waste</u>
- Bookshelf, cabinet, or other storage
- Trash can

<u>Linens</u>
- Throw blanket
- Cushions

<u>Miscellaneous</u>
- Television and video player (Note: not all frugarians would consider this a need)

Basic Dining Room Needs

Based on the articles and advertisements in "house and home" magazines, dining rooms are fancy spaces with hardwood tables, wingback chairs, chandeliers, candles, silverware, and cabinets full of porcelain and crystal. In reality, a dining room is simply the room—or area—in your home where you eat meals as a family. The size and contents of your dining space will depend on your needs and the size of your home. For many of us, the dining room is simply the kitchen table, not a separate room.

Essentially, you need room for each member of your household to sit comfortably for their meals. You may also need a place to store items like placemats, napkins, special-occasion dinnerware, or platters. As we progress through the minimalism stage later in this book, you may find that you don't need a whole sideboard full of dishes for a family of three. Some families inherit furniture or knick-knacks when relatives downsize or pass away. For the most part, we're happy to accept these items (particularly if they're heirlooms), but they don't always match our needs.

The following are examples of basic items needed in a functional dining room:

<u>Electrical and Lighting</u>
- Overhead light or lamps

<u>Furniture</u>
- Table and chairs (one chair per family member)

<u>Storage and Waste</u>
- Bookshelf, cabinet, or other storage
- Trash can

<u>Linens</u>
- Tablecloths
- Placemats
- Cloth napkins

Basic Master Bedroom Needs

The master bedroom is simply the main room where adults sleep. Similar needs would likely be found in other adult bedrooms in the home, particularly if you have elderly relatives or a college-age child living with you. The bedroom holds a special place in the home because it's where we rest—it's where we go to unwind, recharge, and refresh. The key items in a bedroom that allow you to get the rest you need are a comfortable bed and curtains to block out the light.

Although we retire to our bedrooms at the end of the day, they're also where our day begins. As the hub of your personal daily preparedness, most bedrooms should have closet space, storage for clothes, a dresser, and a mirror. The style, décor, and personal touches you add to your space are entirely up to you. By keeping your bedroom furniture to a minimum, you'll be able to invest (whether second-hand or discount retail) in quality pieces that last and can be passed down to other members of your family.

You may also have specific bedroom needs based on your health or personal preferences, such as ambient sound to help you fall asleep or humidifiers and fans to help you breathe. As you assess your bedroom needs, keep in mind the room's actual purpose. It's too easy to use the bedroom for working, reading in bed, or watching television. This not only impacts sleep quality but can also lead to physical and mental clutter, since your space must accommodate all of your non-sleep activities. By stripping your bedroom down to its core function, you'll be better able to start your day refreshed—and with a positive and frugal mindset.

The following are examples of basic items needed in a comfortable bedroom:

Electrical and Lighting
- Overhead light or lamps

Furniture
- Bed frame
- Mattress and boxspring

- Bedside tables
- Dresser
- Curtains
- Chair

Storage and Waste

- Bookshelf, cabinet, or other storage
- Closet or wardrobe
- Hangers
- Trash can

Linens

- Comforter
- Two sheet sets (fitted sheets, flat sheets, pillowcases)
- Mattress pad
- Additional blankets
- Pillows

Miscellaneous

- Laundry baskets or hampers
- Mirror
- Alarm clock

Basic Children's Bedroom Needs

A child's bedroom is similar to an adult's bedroom in its core needs: somewhere to sleep, rest, and prepare for the day. However, a child's needs are somewhat different because children are still in the developmental and formative stages of their lives. A baby or toddler may need a crib for the first couple of years—as they grow, their needs will change to include a larger bed and storage for things like toys, books, and art supplies. Although the primary focus of the bedroom should always be sleeping, older children may see their bedrooms as a place to explore their creativity and as a quiet location to study.

Young children may also need baskets for storage and low shelves for easy access to personal items. A teenager may need a desk and a computer to do their homework. As they enter high school, their bedroom becomes a place of self-discovery and independence, as well as a safe space to cope with the realities of teenage life.

While the basic needs for a child's room are similar across different age groups, as a frugarian, it's important to think about the changing needs of your child throughout their youth. Consider how you can furnish their room so it will grow with them from grade school through college—and maybe even into their first home. Certain pieces could end up becoming heirlooms, such as a toy chest that transforms into a hope chest and is passed down to your future grandchildren.

The following are examples of basic items needed in a practical and comfortable child's bedroom:

Electrical and Lighting
- Overhead light or lamps
- Bedside lamp
- Nightlight

Furniture
- Bed frame
- Mattress and boxspring
- Bedside table
- Dresser
- Curtains
- Chair
- Desk or small table

<u>Storage and Waste</u>

- Bookshelf, cabinet, or other storage
- Closet or wardrobe
- Hangers
- Toy chest or other storage
- Trash can

<u>Linens</u>

- Comforter
- Two sheet sets (fitted sheets, flat sheets, pillowcases)
- Mattress pad
- Additional blankets

<u>Miscellaneous</u>

- Laundry baskets or hampers
- Mirror
- Alarm clock

Basic Laundry Room Needs

Laundry room essentials are pretty straightforward. Whether you have a washer and dryer in your home, a communal laundry room in your building, or use laundromat facilities, there are a few basic requirements for every family to keep clothes clean and help them last as long as possible.

Your specific laundry needs will vary based on whether you have children, the types of clothing you wear for work or leisure, and whether you can make use of the outdoors for hanging garments on a line to dry. You may also need an iron and an ironing board, as well as a laundry room sink if you have garments that require pre-soaking or hand-washing.

The following are examples of basic items needed in a functional laundry room:

Electrical and Lighting
- Overhead light

Appliances
- Washer and dryer
- Iron

Furniture
- Counter or table for folding

Storage and Waste
- Cupboard, shelving, or other storage
- Trash can
- Recycling bin

Miscellaneous
- Backyard clothesline
- Ironing board
- Soaps, detergents, bleach, etc.
- Hangers

Basic Garage Needs

The garage often ends up being a catch-all for many items in the home, especially if you've inherited household goods or furnishings from relatives. A cluttered garage can make your home feel disorganized and non-functional—but a garage that focuses on its primary purpose can be an effective and useful storage space for automotive and garden items, camping gear, bicycles, and sporting equipment.

Even if you don't have a garage, it's important to set aside some space in your home for emergency supplies, household surplus, and tools. This will make home maintenance easier and ensure easy access to items like batteries, candles, and extra stored water during emergencies.

The following are examples of basic items needed in a functional garage:

Electrical and Lighting
- Overhead light
- Flashlight
- Electrical outlet

Furniture
- Counter or workbench

Storage and Waste
- Shelf, cabinet, or other storage
- Storage totes with lids (clear totes preferred)
- Hooks
- Trash can
- Recycling bin

Tool Box
- Toolbox
- Tape measure
- Hammer
- Drill with interchangeable bits
- Nails and screws in a variety of sizes
- Box cutter
- Needle-nose and vice-grip pliers
- Medium-sized wrench

- Wire cutters
- Level
- Straight edge
- Rubber mallet
- Wood glue
- Spackle and putty knife
- Pencils and a sharpener
- Painter's tape
- Masking tape
- Electrical tape

Emergency Supplies
- Water (one gallon per person per day for several days for drinking and sanitation)
- Food (at least a 3-day supply of non-perishable food)
- Battery-powered or hand-crank radio and a NOAA Weather Radio with tone alert
- Flashlight
- First-aid kit
- Extra batteries
- Cell phone with chargers and a backup battery
- Prescription medications and glasses
- Infant formula and diapers
- Cash and change
- Fire extinguisher

Yard Maintenance Supplies
- Mower
- Rake, shovel, and hoe
- Broom and dustpan
- Handsaw

- Pruning shears
- Hedge trimmer
- Hatchet and/or axe
- Garden hose and sprinkler

<u>Vehicle Supplies</u>
- Window scraper
- Antifreeze
- Motor oil
- Booster cables
- Jerry can
- Extension cords
- Roadside emergency kit

<u>Home Maintenance</u>
- Paint, paintbrush, and paint trays
- Ladder or step stool
- Lightbulbs
- Batteries
- Work gloves

Basic Basement Needs

The basement falls into a similar category as the garage, since it's a great place for storage and stockpiling, and tends to become a collection point for many random items. It can sometimes feel as though the bigger your basement, the more junk it accumulates. Since basements tend to be cooler than the rest of the house, they're an ideal storage location for home-canned goods. They're also the perfect spot for a chest freezer or two for bulk perishable items and batch-cooked meals.

The following are examples of basic items needed in a functional basement:

<u>Electrical and Lighting</u>
- Overhead light
- Flashlight

<u>Furniture</u>
- Counter, table, or workbench

<u>Storage and Waste</u>
- Shelf, cabinet, or other storage
- Storage totes with lids (clear totes preferred)
- Hooks
- Trash can

Basic Home Office Needs

A home office doesn't need to be a separate room in your home—it can be any space set aside for work purposes. I personally have a small room for reading, writing, and watching TV that I converted into my home office during the pandemic. It was a tight squeeze, and sometimes it felt like I was always working, because my respite was also my workspace. However, I made do with what I had, and I'm grateful that I could fit everything I needed into that room.

Hubby still works from home, and he uses the living room as his office because he needs space for his computer equipment. Would it be more convenient for him to have his own room so the living room could be used for its actual purpose? Sure—but we live in fairly tight quarters, so we make do with the space we have.

All home offices need a desk or table where you can put your laptop or set up your desktop computer. Depending on the type of job you have, you may need a landline or mobile phone for business communications. You'll also need a chair and some shelving or cabinet space for storage. As you think about your home office needs, consider repurposing items you already have in your home. If you find you need items to make your office complete, try Freecycle for desks and bookshelves, or thrift stores for office chairs and equipment like hole punches, binders, and file organizers.

The following are examples of basic items needed in a practical and comfortable home office:

Electrical and Lighting
- Overhead light
- Desk lamp
- Internet and cable outlets

Furniture
- Desk or table and chair
- Carpet or chair mat

Office Equipment
- Computer and monitor
- Printer (Note: not all frugarians would consider this a need)
- Telephone

Storage and Waste
- Bookshelf, cabinet, or other storage
- Trash can

Health and Safety
- Personal locking safe

Miscellaneous
- Office supplies (notebook, calendar, printer paper, pens and pencils, etc.)

Part 4
Minimize and Organize

Minimalism
What Is Minimalism?

Minimalism is the backbone of the frugal lifestyle. Essentially, minimalism is about assessing and arranging your surroundings to be as simple as possible—freeing your mind from the burden of *stuff* such as:

- The stressful job you need to earn money to buy stuff
- Surrounding yourself with stuff that is not yet paid for and serves as a constant reminder of your debt
- Hoarding stuff inherited from others because of memories, sentimentality, or a sense of obligation
- Suffocating your physical space with stuff that serves no useful purpose other than to display your "wealth" to others

Minimalism is becoming increasingly popular, even outside the frugal lifestyle. In an effort to find balance and harmony, the art of assessing personal objects can help you determine which items are worth making room for—both in terms of physical footprint and mental headspace.

Minimalism isn't just about reducing the amount of material goods in your home—it's an overall attitude of freeing yourself from situations, experiences, events, and goods that clutter up your life. Removing the chaff of consumerism will allow the flower of frugality to flourish!

The following questions will help you minimize by understanding your needs, organizing your space, and offloading your unneeded surplus. As you approach minimalism and work through each item in your home, consider:

- Is it something you currently use?
- When was the last time you used it?
- What do you use it for?
- How often do you use it?
- How many of the same item do you have?
- Do you own something similar that can perform the same function?
- Does it have sentimental value?
- Is it something a family member or friend might need?
- Is it in suitable condition to donate to charity if not needed?

Minimalism, when practiced as a frugarian, differs slightly from traditional minimalism. It requires balancing two complementary yet sometimes conflicting ideals—living only with what you need or what brings fulfillment, and maximizing the value of what you already own to avoid waste.

This balance can be challenging. Frugarians strive to minimize possessions to what's essential in the present, while also keeping certain items that may be useful in the future. As a new frugarian, I recommend approaching minimalism gradually. Use up what you already have—like those half-empty bottles of shampoo under the bathroom sink—before discarding or replacing them. By viewing your environment through both minimalist and frugal lenses, you can make the most of what still holds value while maintaining a space that feels intentional, functional, and comfortably simple.

Although I'm a strong advocate of minimalism, I can admit it's not for everyone. Some people find comfort in surroundings filled with objects. Others have difficulty letting go and reconciling the original cost of an item—even though it no longer serves a purpose. As a frugarian, you're not obligated to be a minimalist. You should, however, look at what you have through a minimalist lens—it will help you identify items in your home that aren't actually needs, wants that no longer have value, and *stuff* that no longer positively impacts your life.

Why Minimize?

There are many reasons people embrace minimalism, and each individual has their own. For frugarians, it's mainly a means to an end—a tool for sustainable frugal living. In this way, the concept of minimalism fits like a keystone into the framework of frugality.

Frugal Foundations

- **Paradigm shift.** Minimalism can spark a mindset change for new frugarians. Moving away from items that crowd your physical, mental, and spiritual spaces helps you see that happiness doesn't come from *stuff*. The moment you place the first item in a donation pile often brings relief and satisfaction, while turning your surplus into a benefit for others.
- **Save money.** By understanding what you already own, how often it's used, and whether you truly need it, you can reduce unnecessary future purchases. As you minimize each room, take time to assess duplicates, clear out hidden items, and resell surplus to reclaim money spent. Those funds can then be put toward organizational tools like containers, shelves, or cabinets.
- **Save time.** A minimized home is often the most efficient because everything has its purpose and place—both physically

and mentally. Knowing where items are, or being able to find them easily because they aren't buried under clutter, saves you time and reduces stress.

- **Fewer distractions.** There's nothing like walking into a room and having space to breathe, think, and move. When everything has its place, purpose, and value, moving through your home becomes calmer and more enjoyable. Just like a workplace, a home with streamlined spaces promotes focus, mental clarity, and peace.

- **Improved sleep.** Decluttering your space clears both mental and physical stressors, creating a bedroom that invites rest. Think of a sparse, airy hotel room—it's designed for sleep. Your bedroom works the same way: when it's focused on rest, your mind and body will follow, instead of getting distracted by a TV, exercise equipment, or other clutter.

- **Increased mobility.** Fewer possessions in your home means more room to live—and easier relocations when circumstances demand it. Whether due to a job change or family situations, having only what you truly need (plus sentimental or personally valuable items) makes moving into a new home less stressful and more manageable.

- **Reduced environmental impact.** Minimalism helps curb overconsumption by keeping only what's needed, plus a few select wants. Less clutter and fewer impulse buys reduce waste and promote a more sustainable lifestyle. In the U.S., consumption also generates enormous waste—4.9 pounds per person per day (3).

- **Encourage others.** Stepping into a tidy, organized space is both calming and inspiring. By embracing minimalism, you naturally model the benefits of frugal living to friends and family— showing that relationships, experiences, and community matter more than material clutter.

- **Make it a game.** Minimalism isn't a punishment—it's a strategy. Turn it into a personal challenge: before bringing anything new home, ask yourself, "Do I really need this? Why do I want it? Will it last? What can I let go of to make room?" There's no scorecard, but every mindful choice is a small victory for your space and your peace of mind.

Minimizing Spaces

Kitchen

Minimizing items in your kitchen can be surprisingly cathartic. Think about how many times you've shuffled through a packed junk drawer, searching for something you could never find. How often have you opened the cupboard of plastic storage containers, only to have all the mismatched lids come tumbling down? Or reached for one of your dozens of plates instead of tackling the dirty dishes already in the sink?

Minimalism in the kitchen may seem a bit counterintuitive, especially when we reflect on the earlier "needs" section. While there are many things in the kitchen that frugarians would consider essential, there are typically a lot of items that should either be reallocated to the appropriate area of your home (like the tools in the junk drawer), treated as surplus, or donated.

The kitchen tends to be a place that accumulates random items and acts as a cemetery for unused appliances, dishes, and cutlery. This overabundance of kitchen items is often the result of combining lives, inheriting items from a family member, or downsizing from a home with more storage space. When Hubby and I moved in together, we each came into the relationship with very little stuff. What we have now, we accumulated over the years together—but it's often the case that you end up with doubles (or more) of many common kitchen items. I once heard of a couple who tackled minimizing their kitchen, only to discover more than thirty coffee mugs and multiple complete sets of dishes.

As you minimize your kitchen, take care to notice whether your surplus items could be used to meet a future need. Are you setting up a mother-in-law suite for an aging parent? Is your child moving out on their own for the first time? You may find that you have more than enough to meet the needs of your household while also being able to help others in the process.

Bathroom

The bathroom tends to be a catch-all for everything to do with health and beauty (with the occasional screwdriver or lightbulb lurking in the bottom drawer). One of the easiest ways to minimize the bathroom is to take everything out of the drawers and cabinets and replace only the items you actually use as part of your daily, weekly, and monthly routines. This will help you recognize things that are merely taking up space instead of being useful. The needs of each family member will vary, and the organization section can help you determine how best to arrange your space so that individualized bathroom items—like deodorant, shaving kits, makeup, and so on—are easily accessible to whoever needs them.

Minimizing the bathroom is also an opportunity to assess your bathroom linens. Some of us fall into the trap of collecting too many towels and facecloths over the years—buying new before the old are worn and not discarding the old as we replace them. In the case of my Grammie, she had a huge bathroom linen closet that smelled musty, like mothballs, as soon as it was opened. She had bathroom linens dating back to the 1950s, but they were never in regular rotation because they were stuffed at the very back. As she got older and her mobility declined, we worked to make life easier for her by minimizing her space. Many of her bathroom linens were unusable due to the way they had been stored for decades. Once we went through and separated the ruined ones (which we cut up to use as rags), she was able to better enjoy the newer, fresher linens because they were uncluttered and accessible.

Most of us like to have a bit of décor in the bathroom to brighten the space and add character to an otherwise practical room. Hubby and I have had the same décor in our bathroom since we met, and it came with him when we moved in together. We have four small pictures of woodland scenes (ducks on a lake, a moose near a river, a wolf baying at the moon, and a bear grasping a salmon) in cherry-wood-stained frames. He bought them for $10 each at Zellers (the Canadian equivalent of Target). We'll likely use the same pictures forever— they're simple, traditional, classic—and we like them! Other than that, we have a decorative shower curtain and a coordinating bath mat. We don't collect or display knick-knacks, and find the bathroom much easier and quicker to clean without having to move and dust a bunch of individual objects.

As you minimize your bathroom, think about which items can be used communally, what you want to keep extras of (we always have extra adhesive bandages because we're clumsy), and what might look nice displayed on the counter. I buy a special soap with gorgeous Victorian filigree packaging, so I store it on the counter as a decorative item, freeing up space in the cabinet for other things.

Living Room

When I think about minimizing the living room, I immediately start considering the purpose of the room. The living room is a gathering place. It's where families spend the most time together and where we entertain and commune with friends. For some of us, it's where we work or pursue hobbies. It's our movie theatre, our classroom, and our sanctuary. The space has to be comfortable and fulfill the specific purpose for your particular household. Our living room consists of two La-Z-Boy recliners, a small side table, a big-screen TV, speakers, and Hubby's technical equipment for his work-from-home job (as well as his desk and bookshelf). The centrepiece is a massive decorative mountain painting that we bought off Kijiji for $40. For us, this setup is ideal—it allows us to enjoy the movie-going experience in the comfort of our home for a fraction of the price, while still giving us space to host and entertain. It also allows us to hook our TV into the computer so that we can use YouTube and access the library's free streaming services for most of our entertainment needs.

As a frugarian, I'm always on the lookout for dual-purpose furniture like an ottoman with a lift-up top, a side table with extra drawers, or even an entertainment centre with additional storage. We have a banquette seat with storage where we keep all of our canning materials for the season—it frees up space in our home because we don't use them very often.

As you approach minimizing your living room, think about which items you've used in the past year. Look in every drawer, on every shelf, and in every nook and cranny to make sure you're taking every item into account. We all have things we've forgotten about. Even though they're out of sight—stashed away, hidden in the bottom drawer, or sitting at the back of the closet—they can still clutter and burden your mind.

Dining Room

The dining room tends to be one of those places that accumulates a lot of inherited items, such as plates, dishes, china, crystal, silverware, candlesticks, sideboards, china cabinets, and sometimes even large dining tables with several chairs. Your family may need a large dining room, particularly if you entertain big groups of family and friends, homeschool, or enjoy crafting or family game nights. Other families may prefer a smaller dining room because they don't need those items or don't have the space. Minimizing your dining room is an opportunity to think about your family's needs, your social calendar, and which items you actually use.

When you start minimizing your dining room, think about holidays and how the needs for those special occasions fit into your day-to-day. If you have a set of dishes reserved for holidays that feature sleighbells and holly branches, it's worth considering whether you truly need them in your home. If they hold sentimental value and you want to keep them, try putting them into more regular rotation so you can enjoy the memories they bring more often. The same idea applies to other dishes and linens. Do you really need 15 vintage tablecloths inherited from your grandma if the only time you use one is on Thanksgiving? In that case, you can minimize your collection by keeping the most beautiful piece—or the one with the strongest memories or sentimental value. That way, you'll cherish it more often, while donating the other pieces so others can enjoy them as well.

Master Bedroom

As I mentioned earlier, improving sleep is one of the main benefits of minimizing the bedroom. However, it's also an opportunity to free up storage space for seasonal clothing and bed linens and any stockpiled sundry items you may have. In our master bedroom, we've minimized it to the point where there is space in the closet for seasonal clothing, bins for surplus blankets, pillows, and pillowcases, and room to store some of our stockpiled bathroom items, such as Epsom salts and boxes of tissue. If your bedroom is organized well and minimized to only those things that you need or that have value, you may find you have quite a bit of extra storage space in your closets—particularly if you adopt a capsule wardrobe.

Colours can also have a big impact on how minimized a space feels. When you're considering minimizing your bedroom, think about whether you have furniture elsewhere in the house that may serve the same purpose—but is in a more neutral or calming colour. This is also a good opportunity to look at the artwork in your home and see if there are pieces that are more conducive to peace, meditation, reflection, and rest, which you could move to the master bedroom.

Child's Bedroom

The approach to minimizing a child's bedroom is much the same as for other teen and adult bedrooms—but it's important to be mindful of the changing needs of your child as they get older. As you minimize their room, strive to create an organized, spacious, and easy-to-clean space that encourages their ongoing learning, development, and growth. Keep in mind that minimalism isn't about painting the entire room white with white carpet, grey pillows, and beige comforters—that type of minimalism is more of a designer style than a lifestyle anyway. A minimalist room can be full of whimsy and colour!

In a child's room, the more open and clear it is, the safer it will be. An uncluttered room also provides space to set up a small table and chairs or a desk for the child to play and do crafts. As they get older, they can transition that area into a space for homework or computer use. Creating a minimized room for your child will not only make it easier for you to clean, but it will also make it easier for your child to help you. It's an opportunity to instill in them the concept of "everything in its place". If their space is well-organized and stripped back to the basics, it will become second nature for your child to know where items belong and to appreciate what they have—rather than being surrounded by a surplus of toys and other items they take for granted and rarely interact with.

Laundry Room

You may not think there's much to minimize in a laundry room, but this area is often more under-utilized than overcrowded. Minimizing the laundry room involves thinking about how you can maximize the space to make being a frugal launderer easier. This could involve investing in more energy-efficient machines. It could mean going full "pioneer" and using a washboard and basin (many frugarians do laundry that way—I'm not ready to give up my Maytag yet!). It's also an opportunity to set up tools that make laundry day a more frugal endeavour. Consider investing in large, sturdy hooks for hanging clothing and a foldable drying rack for delicate items. Minimalist laundry can even extend outdoors, with open-air wash lines. In the summer, nothing is better than crisp, fresh linens dried on a line—especially in lilac season.

The laundry room is also a great place to store your surplus cleaning supplies and items you may use less frequently, like a mop and bucket or an ironing board. Moving the majority of your household cleaning supplies into the laundry room will also help free up the kitchen and pantry for more food and small appliance storage. If you have children, storing cleaning supplies centrally in the laundry room can make it easier to lock up that space and keep them away from little hands.

Garage

The garage is one of my favourite rooms to minimize. To me, exploring a stuffed garage feels like diving into a big treasure chest full of forgotten items waiting to be reimagined as something useful again. It's also one of the first rooms I recommend tackling when you begin to minimize, since many of the items in the rest of your home would be better suited for an organized space in the garage. The garage is a great place to store things like tools, gardening and yard maintenance supplies, sporting goods, and car items—it's also an ideal long-term storage area for non-perishable goods. Having surplus items readily available makes it easier to plan your monthly shopping trips and restock anything you're running low on.

Minimizing the garage can be daunting because it's usually stuffed to the brim with stuff. The sheer volume of things in your garage can be overwhelming, and it can be tough to know where to start. Minimizing the garage as a frugarian also has its challenges because you don't want to throw out things that may be useful later. With that in mind, I recommend starting by throwing away anything that's clearly garbage—items that are damaged, unusable, or spoiled. This first step can help make the space feel less cluttered and easier to work in.

Think about your life as it is now and the items you use day-to-day. It's easy to look at the garage as an area to store memories and nostalgia, but keeping stuff stacked in boxes isn't very practical since it isn't really accessible for regular use. By reflecting on what items you've used in every season over the last couple of years, you can also start to remove items that you may have used in the past (like those cross-country skis from 1974) but will likely never use again.

Take a moment to jot down in your notebook the activities you and your family enjoy. When Hubby and I minimized the garage, our categories looked something like this: gardening, bike riding, hunting and camping, golfing, home repairs, crafting, automotive, and pets. Because our interests have changed over the course of our relationship, some of the activities we were into 15 years ago (like tennis and badminton) no longer matched our lifestyle. We took the time to reassess what we still enjoyed doing, and donated or sold any items that were no longer of use to us. This exercise can be especially useful when looking at kids' stuff in the garage—with the frequent changes in their interests and the prevalence of fads and trends in each age group, there's often a high turnover of what's actually needed and used. Those accumulated items can be repurposed in other areas of the home, shared with friends and family, or donated to a local charity thrift shop.

Basement

Minimizing the basement is similar to minimizing the garage. For some households, the basement functions much like a garage—a dedicated storage space for tools, garden supplies, and other maintenance items. For others, it serves as a family room, a guest area, a fitness space, or a play area for children. Our basement is dedicated to long-term preparedness, where we store bulk pantry items, household goods like toilet paper and shampoo, and other essentials. It's also home to our laundry room.

Regardless of what you currently use your basement for, the concept of minimizing still applies: is the space being used for its intended purpose, and are the items in it useful for fulfilling that purpose?

Minimizing *Stuff*

After you've examined your rooms for ways to minimize their contents, it's time to consider each individual item that fills those spaces. The following considerations can apply to any item in your home, but many of your daily-use items fall into the categories of clothing, accessories, and books.

Clothing

Clothing is one of those things that everyone wears. We wear specific clothing for different seasons, occasions, physical sizes, and preferences for colours and patterns. People dress depending on their moods and wear certain pieces of clothing for work and play. It's because of this diversity in purpose, use, and circumstance that many of us tend to have a *ton* of clothes. This tendency to hold on to clothing long-term is also reflected in the fact that we often keep items from previous points in our lives, instead of focusing on the clothing we need now. Minimizing clothing can be a difficult exercise for frugarians because we want to get the most use possible out of an item before getting rid of it.

As you go through the process of minimizing your clothing, you should ask not only whether a garment still has value for you in the present, but also if it could have value later—for yourself or someone else. Let's use a pair of my favourite jeans from the 1990s as an example. It's been decades since I could fit into them, but they have sentimental value. I want to keep the pants, yet I also recognize that they don't do me any good stuffed in the back of my closet. As part of this process, I reassessed whether those pants would suit a family member or one of my friends—and if no one I knew personally could use them, I would donate them. This thought process can be helpful for you, too, as you assess each item and decide whether to keep it or let it go.

One of the most crucial steps in minimizing your clothing is to actually try each item on. I know this seems like a lot of work (and it is), but there's no point in keeping items that don't fit, are outdated, or you never see yourself wearing again. I notice that oftentimes, minimizing sentimental clothing can't be accomplished unless you actually put the garment on—until you can see for yourself that no matter how powerful you felt in that blazer with the massive shoulder pads, it's time to move on.

I recommend starting small and focusing on one season at a time. If you're currently in the middle of winter, it's a great time to minimize your summer clothing because you can curate your closet to only include those items that you love and that fit. When that season rolls around, you'll save money on clothing because you'll know what you have and which specific items you may need to complete your wardrobe.

As you go through each of your closets or storage spaces, ask yourself the following questions for yourself and each member of your household:

- Do I wear this?
- Will I ever wear it?
- When was the last time I wore it?
- Is this a special occasion piece?
- Does it have sentimental value?
- Is this something I need to wear for my job?
- Could someone else in my family wear this?
- Could any of my friends make use of this?
- Is this something I could swap with a friend?
- Is this something I could donate?
- Is this truly something I could see myself wearing in the future?

Asking yourself these questions as you progress through the process will make it much easier to let individual pieces go.

Shoes, Accessories, and Handbags

If you're anything like me, you probably have a variety of footwear for different occasions and activities. I personally own a couple of pairs of hiking shoes, one pair of sandals, a nice pair of dress shoes, a pair of winter boots, and rain boots. Because of the type of work I do, I can wear whatever shoes I like to the office. Hubby, on the other hand, has far more shoes—ranging from fancy dress shoes and steel-toed boots to duck-hunting shoes and sneakers. Your footwear needs will depend on your hobbies, occupation, and lifestyle, but this phase is your opportunity to decide whether you truly need all the shoes you own.

As you trim your collection, think about whether a single style could meet most of your needs. For example, I have a pair of high-quality hiking shoes that I wear almost everywhere except for formal occasions. I only need that one pair for daily use, plus a couple of seasonal options like sandals for summer and boots for winter. I don't have twenty pairs of daily shoes because they're unnecessary for my lifestyle. If you need dress shoes for work, consider whether one or two pairs would get the job done. Having fewer shoes also means you can buy better quality footwear that's more comfortable and lasts longer.

Handbags are a similar "fashion collectible", often seen as stylish accessories to coordinate with different outfits. But from a minimalist, frugal perspective, you usually don't need more than one or two. As you go through your closet, consider whether each handbag is in regular use. I have one leather purse I've used for the last ten years—I've polished it, repaired it, and even mended the strap by hand. It's perfectly functional, serviceable, and attractive for my needs. I also have a small, classic black purse for rare occasions when I want something a little fancier than my everyday bag. Few women truly need a dozen handbags. If you find you have a surplus in good condition, consider consignment or selling them on a marketplace like Facebook or Poshmark.

The same approach applies to accessories—for both women and men. If you have a hundred ties but only wear three or four regularly, it's a good opportunity to reduce the surplus.

Jewellery is another area to review. Many people approach frugality with simplicity and modesty in mind. As you sift through your collection, think about why you wear each piece, what it means to you, and whether there's a similar one you could let go of. For example, if you open your overstuffed jewellery box and always reach for your grandmother's pearl necklace, you may not need much else—unless there are heirlooms meant to be passed down. Focus on your favourite pieces—the ones you wear consistently or those with sentimental value—instead of keeping a box full of jewellery you never use.

Books

Books are one of those items that seem to end up in every single room in the house (bathroom included). Having a lot of books around can be a good thing, especially when you have children or others in your family who are inquisitive and eager to learn. But books also tend to occupy a large physical footprint and can quickly make a space feel cluttered. Many book lovers also put great emphasis on possessing the physical book itself and maintaining series or large collections.

The task of minimizing books is often the hardest because many of us are attached to the memory of the story, how it made us feel, and the sense that we'd be tossing aside a friend if we ever removed it from our home. But the frugal mentality is based on getting the most value from an item before donating, selling, or discarding it. If you feel that some of your books no longer have value, it may be time to let them go.

Hubby and I never had a large library of books, but we did have far more than we needed. I had a small collection of Canadian and Alberta history books that I used for research in my fiction writing. I had purchased them over the years from garage sales, flea markets, and thrift stores. I never really coveted books, so it was a simple process to go through my collection and remove those with duplicate themes (most of them were history) and keep only the ones I truly needed to support my writing.

As frugarians, Hubby and I are enthusiastic home cooks, with a collection of cookbooks that hold a lot of value to us. By removing the books we didn't need and minimizing the space they take up, we can now more easily enjoy our remaining books because they're accessible and nicely displayed as décor.

If you love books and want to keep a portion of your collection for you and your family to enjoy, consider these questions as you look to minimize them:

- Have I read this yet?
- Is this something I'll ever read (again)?
- How would I rate this book on a scale of 1 to 5?
- Is the content of this book still relevant, or is it out of date?
- Do I have more than one copy of this book?
- Was this book something I inherited or was gifted, or is it something I chose for myself?
- Would I pay full price for this book today?
- Do I have room for it?
- Why do I want to keep it?
- Could I take this book out from the library if I ever wanted to read it again?

As you examine your book collection through the lens of frugality, keep in mind that books can be a wonderful way to entertain your family and encourage learning and creativity. You don't need to remove any that still have value for you, just to meet a goal of "minimizing". But there are opportunities to use free resources, such as the library and book swaps, to keep you and your family engaged without spending money to physically own the book.

Mental Minimalism

Minimalism isn't just about clearing your physical space—it applies to your mental space, too. In today's world, we're constantly bombarded with information, surrounded by technology, and always "available" for others to reach us. These expectations take a heavy mental toll.

We feel pressured to share our lives on social media, respond to every message the moment it arrives, and keep our schedules wide open for whatever comes next. While this level of connectivity has expanded how we learn, work, and entertain ourselves, it has also made it harder to unplug—to rest, reset, and spend time with ourselves and our loved ones.

Mental minimalism is about recognizing the things that clutter your mind and add unnecessary stress, anxiety, or self-doubt. For me, it wasn't until I started focusing inward that I truly embraced the minimalist side of my frugal lifestyle.

Frugal Foundations

- **Embrace single-tasking.** Our world is obsessed with multi-tasking, but we weren't built to do twenty things at once. Technology can be helpful, sure, but it also tricks us into forgetting that we're human, not machines. Workplace stress is a major cause of mental health problems in Canada (4), and focusing on one thing at a time—especially in your non-work hours—can make a huge difference. Single-tasking cuts through the noise, eases anxiety, and helps you actually get things done. As you simplify your life, you might find yourself naturally falling into the habit of focusing on one task at a time.

- **Make time to unwind.** No one likes the feeling of stress, and if your mind is constantly cluttered, it can make it very hard to relax, rest, sleep, or even think clearly. Taking time out of each day (even just ten minutes) can give your mind a break, shift your focus away from problems, and allow you to enjoy some personal peace and calm. YouTube is an excellent resource for guided meditations, ambient music, calming sounds like birds and waves, and even binaural beats that can be soothing when you feel a headache coming on.

Organization

For frugarians, organization is essential—it allows us to see what we have, find it when we need it, and recognize when an item could serve an alternate purpose. Organization helps us shop smart for the things we need and better rotate and manage the items we already own. You may be looking around your home thinking, "I have this organization thing down! My space is already tidy", or maybe, "There's no place for anything, and nothing's in its place!" No matter what stage you're at in organizing your home, there are many frugal benefits to approaching the task with both purpose and functionality in mind.

Why Organize?

- **Save money.** When you arrange your space in an organized way and can see the items you already have on hand, you'll be less likely to purchase things unnecessarily. If storage areas like your pantry and cabinets are organized, you'll be able to rotate your stock when new items come in and easily identify what needs to be used up before it expires. As a frugarian, you can also save money by organizing your home office or garage—it's easier to get motivated to do your own taxes or change your oil when you have tidy, functional spaces to work in.

- **Save time.** When there's a place for everything and everything's in its place, it saves an incredible amount of time. Not only does it make finding things quicker and easier, but you'll also save time and money by not driving to the store to replace things you already have but can't use because you don't know where they are. Organization can also streamline your meal prep, since you'll know which pantry items you already have and which cupboard they're in. It can even save time in your family's daily routine when the items needed to prepare for the day are in designated, familiar places.

- **Reduce stress.** If you're anything like me, trying to find something in a cluttered, disorganized space can cause a lot of stress and anxiety. Looking for keys "in the last place you remember having them" rarely turns up results, and you end up frustrated and annoyed as your stress levels rise. Keeping your home organized will naturally keep tempers at bay and reduce stressful situations—like those frantic questions from your family as they search for an item that's nowhere to be found.

Organizing your space is something you should tackle in stages. Think about the area of your home that is in most need of help. If you work from home, your home office may be the first place you choose. If you want to start cooking more of your meals at home, the kitchen could be where you start. The important thing to remember is that maintaining an organized home as a frugarian is part of the lifestyle. It becomes second nature. Organization is closely tied to both frugality and minimalism because it makes both ideals so much easier to accomplish.

Organizing Your Space

You don't have to be Marie Kondo or Martha Stewart to understand that organization, design, and style go hand in hand. Have you ever walked into someone's home where everything was neat and organized, but also looked really good? Attractive storage solutions—such as decorative baskets used to hold hats, scarves, and mittens by the front door, or clear plastic bins to store pantry staples like flour and sugar—can make it easier to integrate organization techniques in any space.

When organizing your home, consider the items you use most frequently and those that are only used once in a while. Think about the items you want to have close at hand, and those you could store in a tote at the back of the closet. As a frugarian, you also want to consider the items you already have in your home that could be used to organize different spaces. One of the benefits of minimizing is that when you get rid of stuff, there are usually storage containers left behind. Make sure you also check out your local thrift stores or garage sales for inexpensive storage options.

The following items provide frugal ways to keep your space organized:

- **Wicker baskets.** Baskets are a favourite of many frugarians because you can get them inexpensively at thrift stores, they look nice in most home décor, and they're incredibly versatile. You can store rolled-up towels under the bathroom vanity, keep magazines beside your favourite recliner, or arrange smaller baskets in a dresser drawer to neatly store socks and underwear.

- **Fabric boxes.** These collapsible cardboard boxes covered in stiff, decorative fabric (available at stores such as IKEA) are ideal for closets because the fabric exterior won't damage delicate clothing. I use these boxes to store sweaters, scarves, and winter socks. They're also great for shelves in children's rooms because they come in fun colours and often have handles for little hands to grasp.

- **Plastic storage drawers.** Clear plastic storage drawers are ideal for areas of your home where you need to see what's inside without rummaging through. They're perfect for the garage to store screws, nails, and other small items, and they work well in the bathroom for cotton swabs, cotton balls, and bandages. I've even seen them used in the fridge to hold smaller snack items like yogurt cups, cheese strings, and pepperoni sticks. Try your local dollar store, which usually carries a variety of sizes.

- **Plastic totes.** These are perfect for storing items in the basement or garage because they're rugged and have lids, making them easy to move and stack. They come in different colours, but our preference is always to go for the clear ones, since you can easily see the contents inside without having to unstack them to lift the lid. Totes can be found at your local department or hardware store.

- **Furniture.** Furniture is a great option for storage, especially in homes where space is at a premium. Bookshelves are the most common furniture item used for storage, but other pieces can also serve a dual purpose—like a hollow ottoman where throw blankets are stored, or a chest in the kids' room for toys. One of my favourite pieces is a "tall boy" by the front entrance that has overhead storage for baskets, hooks for coats, a bench for sitting while putting on shoes, and a storage area under the seat that holds hats, umbrellas, and reusable grocery bags.

- **Drawer inserts.** These inserts have a variety of individual compartments that work well in areas like the kitchen or bathroom, where there tends to be a variety of smaller items. At your local dollar store, you'll find a selection of drawer inserts in different shapes and sizes that you can group together to customize. We use them in the bathroom to hold hair ties, scrunchies, extra razor blades, dental floss, sanitary pads, and nail clippers. In the kitchen, they're great for things like bag ties, chip clips, rubber bands, and measuring spoons.

- **Hangers.** If you're new to organization and have traditionally used dressers for clothing storage, consider hanging things up in the closet instead—this can free up space in your drawers for other items and make it more fun to get ready in the morning with all of your options hung neatly and organized. Second-hand hangers can always be found for rock-bottom prices at thrift stores and garage sales. If you're buying hangers brand new, go for skinny hangers—they're a great way to save space and give your closet a tidy, streamlined look.

Frugal Foundations

- **Make organization fun.** Organizing your home shouldn't feel like a burden or cause you stress. It should be an enjoyable activity that helps your frugal life run more smoothly in the future. Involve your family in customizing your spaces—kids are great at noticing unused areas for storage.

- **Take your time.** Organization isn't something to rush. As you go through each room, drawer, nook, and cranny in your home, move at a modest pace. Being patient with the process will help you stay focused on each room's needs, give you space to mentally let go of long-held or sentimental items, and allow your creativity to shine as you discover unique and useful storage locations for your things.

- **Organize one room at a time.** Going through your home one room at a time is the most efficient way to start organizing. When you progress through the minimalism phase, you'll reduce clutter and gain a clearer understanding of what you have. Starting with one room allows you to focus on that space's needs (and potential) while keeping in mind items in other parts of your home that might be better organized if stored there.

- **Start with the most organized room first.** When you think about organizing your space, it's tempting to tackle the biggest problem area first. This sounds great in theory, but it can leave you feeling stressed and overwhelmed. By starting with the "easiest" room first, you'll see that you already have some organizational habits. You'll enjoy a few small successes—and a boost of confidence—when you see how efficient, functional, and light your living space can feel with just a little reshuffling.

- **Organize one storage area at a time.** When organizing a room, it can be tough to know where to begin. Try starting with one dresser, cabinet, bookcase, or closet at a time. Take the cluttered bookcase in your office, for example. If you remove everything and place it in a pile on a table or the floor, and dust off the shelves, it's ready to accept a newly organized and curated collection of items.

- **Group similar items.** Another popular way to approach organization is to gather your belongings into piles of "like" things. For example, you could stack books in one pile, decorative items in another, and personal papers in a third pile. This exercise not only makes it easier to see everything you have, but it also gives you a chance to consider changes that could make your items more useful, accessible, and easy to find. Once items are grouped, you can decide whether they belong together permanently or if some could be relocated, donated, or discarded to create a more efficient and satisfying space.

- **Decide what will go where.** Look at your piles and consider whether they belong back in the same space or would be better suited to another location or storage area in the house. Once you've decided what goes where, move each item to its new home.

- **Mix and match storage solutions.** One of my favourite failsafe ways to approach frugal organization is to mix and match your storage items. If you've ever browsed Pinterest, you know how decorative storage can be when coordinating items are used in the same space. For frugarians, this is a win-win—not only does mixing and matching make decorating foolproof, but it also allows us to take advantage of items found at garage sales, thrift stores, and clearance bins because we're being mismatched on purpose. In my she-cave, I have a red, pink, and floral theme in my decorative items and chose "matching" boxes, shelf organizers, and bookends with similarly coloured flowers in slightly different patterns. They're the same general style but were purchased separately, second-hand, and at a fraction of the price of an actual matching set.

- **Keep daily-use items accessible.** As you organize each room and storage space, consider the items you and your family use most in your day-to-day lives. These are the items you'll want to keep as handy as possible. Just as you wouldn't want to put your most-used pans at the very back of your kitchen cabinets, you also wouldn't want to store your shaving cream at the bottom of a basket under the bathroom sink. The more you think about your daily-use items, the easier it will be to make sure they're always within reach. This also helps prevent overbuying items you didn't realize you already had, because they truly become out of sight, out of mind.

- **Use tags and labels.** If you're new to organization, tags and labels are a great way to keep your space organized—especially since they reinforce the concept of "everything in its place". Labels are particularly helpful if there are children in your home, as they can teach kids where things go and make the tidying-up process engaging, effective, and fun. We don't label everything in our home, but we do label containers of bulk pantry items and large totes of seasonal items in the garage.

- **Get creative.** Look for underutilized spaces in each room of your home. This exercise can be especially useful for those of us with limited space. Take a look at your walls to see if there's room to hang a cabinet or add a bookshelf for extra storage. Look under the furniture to see whether there's enough space for a low-profile basket or a slender plastic tote. There may be more places for storage around your home than you think!

Surplus

The *stuff* that's left over after you've identified and met your basic needs is your surplus—and for frugarians, it can be surprisingly hard to let go of. The key is to keep only things you can realistically see yourself using in the future, and to regularly reassess your stash to make sure it still aligns with your needs. Being wisely frugal also means knowing when to release what no longer serves a purpose, or when you have more of something than you could possibly use before its usefulness runs out (or it expires).

One of the most rewarding parts of organizing and decluttering is giving your surplus items a second life. Whether you share, donate, or sell, there are countless ways to ensure your surplus doesn't go to waste. From swapping clothes with friends or donating to local charities to having a garage sale or flea market table, thoughtfully decluttering your surplus clears your space, supports your community, and reduces your environmental impact.

Frugal Foundations
- **Share surplus with others.** We recently did our annual spring cleaning and had some surplus items that we shared with my sister. They weren't "junk"—just things we no longer had a use for, including an old BBQ and a cat-scratch tree. You can also turn surplus-sharing into a social event where friends and family come by and grab what they want from your surplus pile. This works particularly well for larger items that you can store in your garage temporarily. Freecycle is also a good option if you want to share with people outside of your social circle. Google "Freecycle", along with the name of your city, for options in your area.
- **Donate surplus to charity.** Charitable donations are one of the best ways to relieve yourself of surplus. Not only are you helping

the charity earn money by reselling your stuff, but you're also helping make those items accessible to others who may not be able to afford them brand new. Donating your surplus to charity also perpetuates the cycle of frugality, since you're making second-hand items available for other frugarians to purchase. Giving quality used items to charity instead of throwing them out also helps keep usable items out of the landfill. Our favourite place to donate is Goodwill because they have a program in place to hire people with special abilities and ease them into the workforce. We also donate to the Salvation Army, Savers/Value Village, and local faith-based charity shops.

- **Hold a garage sale.** Who doesn't love a good garage sale? Making up the signs with the kids, setting up the tables with all your surplus items, and dusting off your old fanny pack to have your float of coins and bills at the ready. Garage sales are the most frugal way to get rid of your surplus items because you're making extra cash at the same time as decluttering. Those funds can then be used to pay down debt, set aside for a financial goal, or do something special with your loved ones. Since you're still in your minimizing and organizing phase, you can also buy more storage containers to help with home organization. When promoting your garage sale, don't forget about social media sites like Facebook Marketplace, Kijiji, and Craigslist.

- **Dispose of surplus.** Disposal of your unusable and unwanted surplus items is the final step in this phase. As a frugarian, throwing things away is always a last resort and shouldn't be done without a quick mental check to make sure there's no way anyone could make use of the items. As much as we strive to save and preserve, some things are just garbage. Where you dispose of items will depend on what they are, but in our experience, we take anything that isn't garbage but isn't really sellable (like old wrapping paper, loose scraps of paper, cardboard boxes, packing materials, etc.) to the ReUse centre, where they're sold by the pound. For anything electronic (computers and parts, software, batteries, etc.) or hazardous (cleaning chemicals, paints, solvents, etc.), we take it to the eco-station, where it can be disposed of safely. For true garbage, we either order a junk bin (depending on how much we have or the size of the items) or dispose of it with our regular weekly trash. Check out your community hub for "Big Bin" days, when your city or town provides large dumpsters for people to drop off household and yard waste.

Part 5
Frugal Finances

There's a quiet satisfaction that comes with realizing that frugality gives you the freedom to stay debt-free, live comfortably within your means, and set clear financial goals. Settling into the frugal lifestyle helps you better understand and identify your wants and needs—and be more discerning about how you spend your money on both. Not long after adopting this way of life, you'll naturally start viewing your personal and household finances through a frugal lens.

Debt is everywhere in our society—long-term mortgages, financed cars, vacations, toys—the list of wants is endless. But as a new frugarian, your main goal after meeting your basic needs should be to become and stay debt-free. Most people don't think twice about a 30-year mortgage, but most frugarians would feel uneasy carrying three decades of debt.

As you work through the budgeting exercises in this section, you'll start noticing expenditures that aren't truly frugal or necessary. But it's important to remember that living frugally doesn't mean denying all of your wants or living without the things you enjoy. It's simply understanding that spending money unnecessarily leaves you with fewer funds saved toward your financial future—including the occasional splurge or indulgence.

None of the advice in this section is tied to a specific income level. These tips are general and can be used by anyone seeking to adopt a frugal mindset.

A Penny Saved...

You probably remember the saying our parents and grandparents used to repeat often: "A penny saved is a penny earned". I never gave it much thought until I entered the workforce after college, earning minimum wage in a difficult and often thankless job. That's when I began to truly understand the cost of things in relation to my effort and time. Now, when I consider a "want", I think about how many hours of work it would take to afford it. Trust me—it makes you take pause, especially if you're not particularly fond of your job.

A penny is saved whenever you make do with what you have, choose to do without, or avoid living beyond your means by going into debt. For many of us, our first savings were literal pennies from an allowance or money earned from early jobs like babysitting or shovelling snow. There was a unique satisfaction in hearing those coins clink into a mason jar or piggy bank, set aside for a special purchase in the future.

That feeling is much the same when you follow a frugal budget and see a surplus at the end of the month—even if it's only a couple of dollars. By making conscious decisions not to buy things before they're needed, you naturally shift your mindset toward getting the most use out of every item. Take prescription eyewear, for example. I've personally used the same frames daily for the last twelve years. I could have bought new frames every couple of years, using insurance to offset some of the cost. Instead, I used my benefits for eye exams and had new lenses cut to fit my existing frames. Since I didn't buy frames to match the new lenses each time the prescription changed, it was as if I had "earned back" what I would have spent on a new pair.

Budgeting

Creating a budget and sticking to it is one of the most basic goals of frugality—yet it's also one of the most challenging. Some people tend to be very organized with their finances, while others can be spendthrifts, not really accounting for where their money is going throughout the month. The importance of budgeting your monthly money is the same whether you're a student, part of a family, or on your own. It doesn't matter if you operate on a lower income or a higher income.

A budget can help students identify their semester expenses and determine whether they need a part-time job to make ends meet. It can also help a large, one-income family allocate what they need each week while building in goals for an emergency fund, education savings, and family activities. Budgets can show a single person—in black and white—that they have room in their budget to buy a small house instead of renting. They can enable people with lower incomes to stretch their funds over the whole month and even set aside a small amount for savings. Budgets can allow larger-income families to set aside part of their monthly surplus for larger financial goals and charitable giving.

A common perception of creating a budget is that it's complicated and that you need to be a genius in math to figure it out. Budgeting is as easy as money coming in versus money going out—and striving to end each month with a positive balance. Budgets are most often broken down into fixed expenses and variable expenses.

Fixed Expenses

Fixed expenses are essentially your monthly needs—things you need to survive that have roughly the same cost each month throughout the year. These include expenses like your rent or mortgage payments, cell phone, car payment, or bus pass. An expense is "fixed" because you know an expected amount will come out of your bank account regularly, so you need to have the money available to cover it.

Variable Expenses

Variable expenses are those that change or vary throughout the month and fluctuate based on how much you buy. Consider lunch on a workday. You may have $25 per week budgeted for lunch, but that expense can change at any time, depending on how much or how little you spend. If you only spend $15, you'll have a $10 surplus at the end of the week. But if you spend $30, you'll have to spend $5 less next week, dip into savings, or go into debt if you don't have the additional funds available.

Since you're in control of how much you spend each week, variable expenses are the items in your budget with the most frugal potential. For instance, a frugarian may allow themselves the same $25-per-week budget but choose instead to pack their lunch most days to keep costs low. One of our favourite meals is a big homemade pizza—and there are always a few pieces left over. Those extra slices become the next day's lunch and save me the cash I would have spent in the cafeteria. When you pack your own lunch, you're earning back money to put into your savings or toward building your stockpile of food.

Groceries are another great example. A family of four might have an $800-per-month food budget and set a goal to reduce that by $100 through shopping sales, meal planning, and batch cooking. That surplus could then be used to build up their emergency fund or set aside for larger financial goals. Other variable expenses include vehicle fuel, utilities, gifts, and personal and family activities.

Each Piece of the Pie

When you're starting a budget, one way to think about the breakdown of expenses is like pieces of a pie. The whole pie represents the total amount of your family's take-home pay, which is your *net* income. The amount of money that makes up your pie isn't the important part—it's how you divide the pie that matters. According to the U.S. Census Bureau, families should allocate no more than 30% of their net monthly income to housing (5). Housing expenses aren't limited to your rent or mortgage—they include all expenses that relate to your housing needs, such as insurance, property taxes, and condo fees. They also include your contingency or maintenance fund for unexpected costs like a blown water heater, a new furnace, or roof repairs.

Food

Food is the next largest piece of the pie, and it's recommended that you allocate approximately 15% of your net income to this need (6). This slice of your budget isn't just for groceries—it also includes all those trips to fast-food places, orders from delivery apps, and evenings out at your favourite restaurants. Everything you eat or drink should come out of this piece of the pie. The more often you eat at home, the more money you'll save. That surplus can then be used to buy better-quality ingredients, a greater variety and quantity of food, and gardening tools and supplies to start cultivating your own sustainable food source.

Transportation

Transportation is the next biggest piece of your expenses pie. This piece is made up of car payments, insurance, registration, gas, maintenance, and contingencies like car repairs or accident liability payments. It also includes alternate transportation expenses, such as cab fare, rideshare apps, and new tires for your vehicle or bicycle. Ideally, transportation should be no more than 15% of your net income (7). It's also a variable expense, so the more frugal you are with how you get around, the more you can save or reallocate to other slices of your budget pie.

Utilities

Another large piece of your budget is utilities, with expenses including heat, water, power, sewage, septic, internet, and cell phone. Some of these items are fixed, where the cost is largely the same month to month. Others are variable, and their cost can be reduced by limiting your consumption and use. Adopting frugal habits—like washing your clothes in tap-cold water or opening the curtains for sunlight and warmth during the day—can add up to big savings in your overall household budget.

Edutainment

In our budget, Hubby and I also allocate 10% of our net income to "edutainment", a term we use for things that could be educational, entertaining, or both. Educational expenses include tuition or course fees, school uniforms, books, art supplies, pens and paper, and computers. Entertainment could be anything from video streaming services to trips to the zoo—whatever you spend money on to keep your family entertained and occupied. Since most of our entertainment is in our home or free when we go out, like walking around our city's urban wetlands or visiting the large downtown library, we tend not to eat up much of this budget slice.

Disposable Income

The remaining piece of your expenses pie is your *disposable income*. This piece should be divided into smaller morsels of debt repayment, cash savings, personal savings, retirement fund, and charitable giving. Debt repayment is a priority and should get the largest portion of your disposable income—more than the monthly minimum payment, if you can afford it. Cash savings is a personal fund for wants. How you spend your cash savings is up to you, even if you want to put it toward other pieces of your pie. Personal savings include your emergency fund, your six-month savings fund, and any savings you have for personal financial goals—like a newer vehicle or a down payment on a home.

Retirement savings is a portion of your disposable income set aside each month for your future non-working life, which, for many people in North America, begins around age 65. Your retirement allocation can be in the form of your work retirement plan, a personal retirement account, or a registered retirement fund through your bank (ideally a combination of the three). Regardless of your income, it's essential to begin preparing for your retirement years as early as possible by setting aside a portion of your disposable income every month—even if it's only $5.

The final allocation in your disposable income slice is for charitable giving. Since this is a variable expense, the amount you give is based on what you can afford in any particular month. In my family, we give a modest amount to our local food bank most months. But when there's a month when funds are tight, we may skip our donation. Sometimes, when we have more wiggle room, we might increase our contribution to share more of what we have because of a surplus. Although you aren't obligated to donate *any* of your money, as a frugarian, it's important to practice gratitude and consider those less fortunate.

Plotting Your Current State

Before creating your frugal budget, it's important to take a moment to assess your current financial state. This means gathering all of your financial documents in one location, organizing them by bank and date, and separating them by purpose. For example, sort all of your mortgage documents together, all of your car loan documents together, all of your credit cards together, and any other debts or assets you may have, like investments or retirement savings. Before you can start plotting figures into your budget, you need to know where you stand. I recommend getting financial statements printed by your bank for each of your bank accounts, investment accounts, credit cards, and loans (including your mortgage).

How you choose to create your budget is up to you. Whether you use budgeting software, prefer pen and paper, or want to use a fancy spreadsheet—it's entirely your choice. The important thing is to evaluate your assets against your liabilities before diving into the finer details of each item. Your assets are your hard cash. This does not include money invested in your home because, until it is fully paid off, it's still considered a liability (I understand your home still has equity, but we'll treat it wholly as debt for this exercise). A liability is anything you owe to someone else, in any amount. It could be money owed to the bank on your mortgage or student loan, money owed to a credit card company, or even twenty bucks owed to a friend—they're all debt obligations.

Your primary budget goal should always be to meet the basic needs of you and your family. Once those needs are met, you can begin working toward larger financial goals. As a frugarian, your focus should be to get your assets to a comfortable place and reduce or eliminate liabilities. This means paying off all consumer debt and your mortgage, and striving for an emergency fund of at least $1,000 for short-term expenses like a blown tire or a broken appliance. You should also work toward a fund of at least six months of living expenses—enough to cover food, shelter, utilities, and transportation for your household (8). This fund should only be used in case of a job loss or another unexpected, life-altering event, such as a natural disaster or a family member's illness. Once you're debt-free, any savings will contribute to greater financial freedom in the future.

The goal of this pre-budgeting stage is to get as close to net neutral as possible. For example, if you have $5,000 owing on several credit cards, a $1,000 emergency fund, and $3,000 in your savings account, you have the potential to pay off your smallest debts first and reduce your monthly payments. Those saved payments can then be applied to the credit card with the next smallest balance, and so on. There's no point in having money in the bank earning 1% when you have credit card balances with 28% interest.

For most people, this won't be an instant process. Depending on your debt load, it could take several months—or even years—to bring your budget to a balanced state. The important thing to know before you plot your budget is exactly how much money you have versus how much you owe. If you have surplus money that you can put toward your debt, do it as soon as possible and close out those credit cards. Most frugarians rarely use credit cards, and some don't use credit at all. However, there are some things that do require a credit card, like booking flights or hotels. Having a credit card can be useful, but it's essential to be responsible with how you use it.

Measuring your assets against your liabilities will also help you figure out which debts to tackle first and how much of your disposable income to allocate toward debt repayment. Keep in mind that as you pay off your debts, you should eliminate the bills with the highest interest rates first—unless there are debts small enough to be discharged after just a couple of payments. You'll want to eliminate those first.

Debt Repayment

I was in massive amounts of student loan debt for the better part of eight years. When I finished graduate school in 2011, I was $88,000 in debt. It was a heavy feeling. I understood when I decided to go to school that I would be responsible for the cost. I got scholarships, bursaries, and grants, but those only scratched the surface of the annual tuition, books, and fees—not to mention housing, food, and transportation. But I was like a lot of other kids from modest backgrounds who relied on student loans to fund their higher education.

A month or so out of school, I relocated for an entry-level position in provincial government. To discharge my debt as quickly as possible, I dedicated any spare money—even if it was only a few dollars—to paying it down. Was there sacrifice? You bet! But those sacrifices were necessary to achieve the financial freedom I have now. My original loan had an amortization period of 15 years and a monthly payment of $985 CAD. I often made double payments by squirrelling away money during the year, working my side hustle at freelance writing, and forgoing those expensive social events that ensnared my friends (like dinner and drinks for $100 a pop). I didn't even feel like I was missing out because I made different plans with friends that didn't revolve around spending money.

Now that we're debt-free, we can grow our savings much faster because we aren't spending money on interest payments. We pay cash for things we need and always live within our means, even if it means making do with what we have or doing without. Instead of activities that strain our wallets, we focus on home-based entertainment, time in our local parks and playgrounds, and genuine connection with family and friends.

When you approach your debt repayment as a frugarian, consider the following:

- **Prioritize.** Repaying your outstanding debts should be a priority. The idea of paying interest to another party instead of letting it accrue in your own accounts should motivate you to make small, incremental changes in order to afford debt repayment. If you currently carry debt but are still indulging in unnecessary wants, take some time to consider how to best allocate your disposable income. As a frugarian, debt repayment should come first after the basic needs of you and your family are met.

- **Sacrifice.** Prioritizing your debt repayment on paper is the easy part. Putting it into action is much more difficult, since it forces you to assess your current behaviours, what you spend money on, and how you can trim expenses. If you're used to spending $6 a day on a fancy coffee or blowing $50 on drinks each Friday night, prioritizing debt repayment may require some sacrifice. You didn't get into this situation overnight, and just like any dietitian will tell you about losing weight—you won't see changes on the scale until you make changes in your life. Approaching sacrifice with a frugal outlook will help you understand that small changes now will add up to greater savings in the future.

- **Hustle.** Maybe you have a friend who delivers pizza on the weekends, or a relative who sells Tupperware in addition to her full-time mommy duties. Anything you do above and beyond your normal job is a "side hustle". Money earned from part-time or casual work is a great way to quickly pay down debt or save for another financial goal. Depending on your skills, there may be a variety of jobs you could do to earn extra money. I'm a writer, so I make extra money from book sales and also take on freelance copywriting and editing jobs when I have time. Every dollar counts.

Financial Freedom

When you think about financial freedom, you may picture sailing on the ocean or walking through rows of grapevines at a winery, as advertisers show us in those "Freedom 55" commercials. As a frugarian, however, it most often means being free from the burden of debt. It means having the ability to pay for the things you need without using credit.

There's an incredible weight of worry and stress that comes with carrying a debt load of any size—but it's even more troublesome when that debt load is unmanageable month to month. The release when paying off your debt, most importantly, includes mental freedom. There's a calm and steadiness of mind that comes from seeing positive numbers in your bank account. This can take the form of a better night's sleep, less stress, or more positive interactions between you and your family. When Hubby and I became debt-free, there were fewer tense conversations about the strain on our monthly finances caused by our debt load.

For our family, financial freedom also comes in the form of time. Since we're no longer tied to the high-stress, high-paying jobs that were needed to pay off large debts, we can now work modest-paying jobs while still maintaining a positive bank balance. These jobs are not only less stressful, but they have given us back time to spend with family, friends, and each other. They also free up our calendar for volunteer hours and charitable work. No matter what your personal debt load or financial goals are, a healthy financial future is much easier to achieve without the shackles of debt.

Breaking Free From Credit

To help you break free from your reliance on credit, gather all of your credit cards. Identify the card with the lowest interest rate and annual fee, and enough credit room for something like a vacation or minor home repair. Strive to make that card the only one you keep, use it only when required, and pay off the balance as soon as possible. Make a plan to repay all of your debt, starting with the card that has the lowest balance and highest interest rate first. As you pay off each card, call the credit card company and cancel it. Cut it up, and breathe a sigh of relief knowing you've discharged the burden of another debt. Repeat until all of your consumer debt is repaid.

Budget Cuts

One of the main parts of managing your frugal finances is looking for ways to cut items from your budget to free up funds for other things—primarily your debt repayment and other financial goals, like saving for a house or your child's education. Budget cuts are small sacrifices you're willing to make to pay down your debt as a frugarian. Some people new to the frugal lifestyle assume that budget cuts are all about making coffee at home and packing PB&J sandwiches instead of hitting the breakfast cart at work. But while reducing how much you eat out is a great start, most line items on your budget have a little room to trim the proverbial fat.

Financial advisors will often recommend reducing spending on your variable expenses, but frugarians tend to go even further. We assess how to adjust both our fixed expenses and variable spending behaviours to create a balanced and sustainable long-term budget.

Food and Water

Reducing food spending is one of the easiest ways to see savings in your monthly budget. Grocery stores have deals every week, and if you're smart about shopping sales and committed to eating at home, you can see quick gains in your bank account.

Frugal Foundations

- **Eat most meals at home.** If you take a look at your current eating habits, it's likely that you and your family occasionally eat lunch out, grab a snack on the way home, go out on Friday nights, or stop for supper on the go while running weekend errands. Our lives revolve around meal times. In our fast-paced society, many of us fall into the convenience traps of restaurants and takeout, rationalizing the cost because we're "busy".

However, by organizing your kitchen and making it conducive to preparing, cooking, storing, and packing your own food, eating at home will become a welcome and comforting part of your frugal routine.

- **Shop the flyers and use coupons.** We've all seen those TV shows about extreme couponers who combine coupons to get tons of items from the grocery store for free or at steep discounts. While this may be the popular idea of what a "couponer" is, the reality is much more modest. When you base your meals on what's on sale, getting into the habit of using weekly coupons becomes part of your shopping routine—without veering into the extreme. Most grocery stores post their weekly flyers online, and many also offer digital or printable coupons. This allows shoppers to see which items are a good deal and plan their shopping lists accordingly. Some stores even do "loss leaders" or mega sales on select items to draw customers in. Those items are ideal for buying in bulk and adding to your pantry and stockpile.

- **Shop seasonally.** A friend of mine once lamented that her grocery bill was close to $1,000 each month for a family of three. I asked her why her bill was so high. She wasn't sure, but she did reveal that she doesn't shop with a plan—she just buys whatever the family is in the mood for that week, regardless of the cost. That mentality is an easy way to overspend on groceries. By making purchases based on what you want, rather than what's on sale and affordable, you miss out on the great deals and reduced prices that come from seasonal goods. This concept also applies to seasonal sales on items like ham and turkeys around the holidays, or discounts on condiments like ketchup and mustard during BBQ season. Paying attention to how grocery stores reduce prices during and after each season can result in big savings.

- **Shop clearance and sales first.** Grocery stores are always running sales on select goods, and when those items fail to sell within a certain time, they get marked down for clearance. Clearance racks for dry goods and household items are often at the very back of the store, near the entrance to the "employees only" area where stock is received. Meat clearance is usually a small section of the butcher's coolers where individual packs of meat are marked down. Be sure to take caution when buying marked-down meat: if the best-before date is the day you buy it, cook the meat that day or freeze it. If you decide to freeze it, mark the package "Cook same day thawed" to prevent consuming it past its expiry date. Clearance fruits and vegetables are usually on a rack in the produce section—this is a great place to find cheap bananas for banana bread and smoothies, tomatoes for homemade sauces, and overripe fruit for home-canned jams and jellies. The bakery section usually has discounted breads, and they also mark down pastries and desserts daily. If you need a cake for a special occasion, the clearance area is a great option because desserts (especially frosted cakes) stay fresh well past their "best buy" date and are often marked down 50–75%.

- **Meal plan and batch cook.** Meal planning fits perfectly into frugality because it allows you to shop for the most affordable items and base your meals on what's on sale and in season. Take a look through your weekly grocery store flyers—oftentimes, stores group together sale-priced items that can be used to make complete meals (such as a sale on ground beef, spaghetti, marinara sauce, and parmesan cheese in the same week). As a frugarian, pay attention to these types of sales and plan your weekly meals around them. You can also get into the frugal habit of doubling recipes and freezing half for later. Not only does this practice save time and money, but it also makes it much less tempting to order takeout on nights when you're tired and busy.

- **Discover discount stores.** Hubby and I are "foodies". I'm a classically trained chef, and he's a better cook than I am because he has no fear, loves to experiment, and can eat pretty much anything. We love to cook meals together and shop locally for fresh ingredients. At the beginning of our relationship, however, we indulged by frequenting boutique butchers, fine cheese shops, and artisan bakeries. We didn't incur debt shopping at these fancy stores, but when we reflect back on it (which, as frugarians, we often do), we marvel at the amount of money we spent on items that could have been purchased for a fraction of the price at discount food retailers. Grocery stores such as Aldi, Trader Joe's, and No-Frills offer most of the same items as larger chain stores at vastly reduced prices. They often liquidate surplus from manufacturers and higher-end grocers who turn over stock frequently due to packaging changes or discontinued production. These stores don't always carry the same items week to week—but it's a fun treasure hunt to see what's on sale and how we can use it to create unique, delicious, and satisfying meals.

- **Shop at more than one store.** For convenience, most families tend to favour shopping at a single store for groceries and household items. Frugarians, however, follow the sales—even if that means going to more than one grocery store. As you become familiar with flyers and the timing of when items usually go on sale, you'll start to see patterns and cycles. You can build your weekly route based on what's on sale at each location. We recently did our monthly grocery shop at Costco, Save-on-Foods, No-Frills, and Safeway. Because we do our shopping in a circular route, it's not that much driving. We also only shop twice per month. We're able to maximize our savings by scoring the rock-bottom sale items at each of the four stores.

- **Pack lunches and travel snacks.** One of the biggest money-saving food tips for new frugarians is to pack a lunch or snacks when you know you'll be away from home for an extended period. Too often, we think we won't be gone long, or that we'll just pick something up at a fast-food restaurant if our errands run late—but these are just excuses to spend far too much money to satisfy our hunger. Before you or your family members head out for the day, think about which meals will be missed while you're away. For instance, if you're spending Saturday exploring garage sales, why not build a picnic lunch into your plans? Pack a small, soft-sided cooler with an ice pack, simple ham and cheese sandwiches, a few pieces of fruit, and a couple of cookies for each of you. Snacks are also a great frugal item to have on hand—you can even keep them stocked in the car for when hunger strikes. Try making your own snack packs with trail mix, banana chips, or dried fruit to give you a quick boost of energy for shorter trips away from home. With a bit of simple planning, you can save a lot of money on drive-thrus, restaurants, and takeout.
- **Drink water.** The easiest way to save money on food as a frugarian is to stop drinking packaged beverages—especially bottled water. Water is free, tastes great, and is the ideal choice for your health and well-being. Make it a frugal habit to pack reusable water bottles for you and your family whenever you go out. At home, keep a pitcher of cold, filtered water ready in the refrigerator. Thrift stores are an excellent place to find quality

second-hand water bottles. When you're out and about, many public places—such as shopping malls, recreation centres, and schools—have water fountains where you can refill your reusable bottles.

Shelter

For most people, shelter represents the largest slice of their budget pie. It can be challenging to reduce housing costs because of fixed-rate mortgages and rental lease agreements. However, saving on shelter now can help you achieve other financial goals in the future. During your needs assessment, if you determined that you have more space than you need, consider whether downsizing to a smaller place might be a better option. Instead of moving, you could also rent out one of your rooms— or even the basement if it's outfitted with a kitchenette or mother-in-law suite. If you live in an apartment, check with your landlord to see if there are different floor plans within the same building that rent for less. Even a small reduction in square footage could result in a lower monthly payment. By trimming your shelter costs where you can, you'll give yourself more breathing room in the rest of your budget.

Frugal Foundations

- **Refinance your mortgage.** Whether you're on a fixed- or variable-rate mortgage, there may be opportunities to speak with your mortgage broker about refinancing or renegotiating your loan. Refinancing could be an option if you're currently in consumer debt or don't have enough income to cover your monthly expenses and are relying on credit to make ends meet. Although one of your primary goals as a frugarian is to live a debt-free life, that isn't always possible right away. By extending your mortgage term slightly and lowering your monthly payment, you'll free up funds to meet your family's needs and begin transitioning away from filling budget gaps with credit. A term extension is a temporary measure and should only be used as a last resort. Once you're consistently and comfortably meeting your needs—whether through increased income or reduced variable expenses—you can start saving toward lump-sum mortgage payments to pay down that debt more quickly.

- **Renegotiate your lease.** If you're a renter, you're either on a month-to-month payment schedule or have signed a lease. A lease is the ideal arrangement because it allows you to know exactly how much your payment will be each month for a fixed period. If you're looking for a new place to rent, consider options that include utilities. We currently rent a house where all utilities are included—an advantage in a climate like Edmonton, with its incredibly cold winters and unbearably hot summers. If you know you intend to rent for more than a year, try negotiating a longer-term lease for a reduced rate. If you're a good tenant, pay your rent on time, and don't disturb others, your landlord will see you as a valuable part of their investment. Many landlords are willing to lower rents for each additional year a lease is signed in advance. For example, you might currently pay $1,500 per month on a one-year lease but could rent the suite for $1,450 if you sign on for two years. It never hurts to ask—sometimes that simple question can save you hundreds of dollars a year.

- **Rent out a room in your home.** If you're looking for a way to generate income or offset the cost of your rent or mortgage, consider renting out a room in your home. Rentable spaces may include a basement suite, the room above the garage, a spare bedroom, or even the attic. Depending on where you live, there may also be a high demand for short-term housing for students, new arrivals, and transient workers. By setting a fair rate and furnishing the space with simple furniture suitable for basic

adult needs, you can earn a steady bit of extra income—money that could be set aside for savings or used to pay down debt. I lived with my uncle during my first year of college and paid him a modest rent for a furnished bedroom with access to the kitchen, bathroom, laundry facilities, cable, and internet—he even had an adorable cat who was a comfort during exams. In my first couple of years after school, I lived in a boarding house with seven other people. For most young adults, shared accommodation is part of transitioning into independence. Take a look in your local paper for "rooms for rent" or "suites for rent" to see what types of places others are offering and what rates are typical in your area. Also, be sure to check your local requirements for registering the room, and make sure you include any rental income in your annual tax return.

- **Negotiate your insurance rates.** Call your insurance providers to see if there's a better rate for your home coverage. You can also check whether there's an incentive for paying your fees yearly instead of monthly—we saved over 10% by switching from smaller monthly payments to a single annual lump sum. Consider asking about options for combining your home and car insurance, since most providers offer bundle discounts.

- **Downsize into a less expensive residence.** After completing your needs assessment, you should have a clear idea of whether your current home meets your needs or is simply too much house. If your home takes up too much of your budget and offers more space than you need, consider moving into a smaller, less expensive property. Even relocating to a different neighbourhood can reduce your mortgage while maintaining the square footage you need. You might find that you don't need a house at all—condos, townhouses, and apartments are all popular downsizing options.

- **Move to a more rural location.** Moving to a new neighbourhood in your city can be an effective way to downsize your shelter, but an even more frugal option is to move to a smaller town or village. One of our long-term goals is to relocate to a small town about an hour from our current home—a city of over one million people. Houses here are prohibitively expensive, and we worry that if we stay, we may end up among the generation who never owns a home. Even moving slightly outside the city can reduce housing costs substantially. If you're able to work remotely, you can move even farther out and find property and a home for a fraction of urban prices. There's a certain charm and sense of community in small towns, but it's a big leap—social circles can be tight, nepotism can make finding a job challenging, and the range of activities, art, and culture is often far more modest than in urban centres.

- **Welcome your children to live at home while in school.** One of the greatest gifts you can give your children after graduation is the option to live at home while they're in university or trade school. This gives them time to transition out of high school and gain some independence, while still having family support nearby as they step into adulthood. It also offers a buffer against falling into debt and can save you money if you were planning to contribute to their dormitory or meal plan costs.

- **Allow your kids to stay with you after graduation.** If your child has decided not to go to college, a good way to set boundaries and teach financial responsibility is to charge a small rental fee for staying in your home, starting one year after graduation. Allowing them to stay at home rent-free for that first year gives them time to transition into the workforce and, potentially, their own residence. It may seem like taking advantage of your child to charge rent, but I'm not talking

$1,000 a month. Something modest, like $200 per month and an additional $100 toward groceries, can help them understand budgeting, writing cheques, and making sure there's enough money in their bank account to cover their expenses.

- **Make lump-sum mortgage payments.** Depending on the terms of your mortgage contract, you may be eligible to make additional payments toward your loan. Options for additional payments include before or at the end of your term, at select periods throughout your term, or at other times specified in your contract. Be sure to consult your mortgage broker before making any additional payments—some mortgages carry penalties for early repayment.

- **Do it yourself.** One of the biggest expenses for homeowners is renovations and unexpected maintenance. When possible, take the frugal route and do it yourself. This is not to say you should tackle complex trades like plumbing or electrical work yourself (unless you're trained and certified), but for select tasks such as painting, landscaping, and simple tiling, doing it yourself is definitely an option. There are plenty of learning resources available for DIYers—whether you check out books from the library or watch how-to videos on YouTube, you can pick up basic renovation techniques that could save you a bundle.

- **Buy second-hand.** In many cases, saving money on your shelter expenses can be as easy as shopping second-hand. If you're planning home renovations, check out your local Habitat for Humanity Re-Store or ReUse centres, which specialize in recycled, reclaimed, and refurbished building materials— everything from lumber and cabinets to tiles and light fixtures. If you're looking to spruce up your interior with furniture and décor, shop your local thrift stores, garage sales, and online second-hand marketplaces for deals. You can often find unique pieces that add character to your home while keeping your budget on track.

Transportation

Cutting costs on transportation is one of my favourite frugal hacks because you're not only saving cash, you're also improving your health and wellness since many alternative ways of getting around are self-propelled. Reducing transportation expenses can be a challenge for some new frugarians because of the convenience of having a car (or more than one). There's a sense of freedom and independence that comes from being able to hop in your vehicle and drive anywhere. But other than housing, vehicles are the biggest debt most people carry. The interest accrued on a seven-year car loan should make you rethink ever financing a vehicle again.

Since I personally use the frugal option of public transportation, we save on the costs associated with me owning a car—including gas, insurance, repairs, and maintenance. If I need to get somewhere more quickly than a city bus allows, or to an area of the city without transit service, I can call a taxi or have Hubby drive me if he's not working.

Frugal Foundations

- **Pay off remaining debt on financed vehicles.** If you have debt remaining on your car loan, consider using your savings to pay it off. This is only recommended if you have enough savings to cover the loan while still maintaining a minimum $1,000 emergency fund. Once you've paid off your remaining debt, consider making a commitment as a frugarian never to finance a vehicle again.

- **Downsize to a modest, paid-off vehicle.** If you don't have the savings to pay off your vehicle, consider downsizing to a less expensive option. Many of us have been trapped by the "status symbol" of a fancy car without realizing the burden of a giant car payment—it actually takes much of the joy out of owning the car in the first place. As a frugarian, your mode of transportation should be just that: a way to get from one place to another. Used vehicles can be in excellent condition— especially those purchased from a dealership. They're also typically under warranty, with all safety and mechanical checks done before they hit the sales floor. Honestly, you'll wonder why you ever bought brand new. To save money on our transportation costs, we paid cash for a 10-year-old Ford Explorer that's still running smoothly five years later.

- **Create a vehicle maintenance fund for contingencies.** Have you ever had a blowout on the highway and had to call for a tow truck? Or tried to start your car in the morning only to hear the dreaded "chug-chug-thump"? Vehicle issues are often unexpected and *always* expensive. By setting aside a small amount of your disposable income for a "car maintenance contingency fund", you create a buffer—insurance, if you will—against the cost and unpredictability of car repairs. The amount you set aside monthly will depend on your personal savings goals and what you can afford. The important thing is to commit to putting money into the fund each month. In our household, we set aside $50 per month. At the end of the year, we divide the fund in half: half goes into our "future car fund," and the other half rolls over to cover vehicle expenses that may come up in the following year. Even though there will already be money in the fund at the start of the year, it's important to continue contributing until you have an amount that can cover both sudden car repairs and, if necessary, a portion (or all) of the cost of a replacement used vehicle.

- **Walk, bike, or scoot short distances.** If you're looking for the least expensive transportation option, getting around on your own two feet is the most frugal. If you're not used to this type of exercise, start with shorter distances. Try walking a couple of blocks to the corner store, or walking to pick up your kids from the neighbourhood school. Even trying it just a few times per week to start can reduce the amount of money you spend at the gas station.

- **Carpool or rideshare.** One of the most effective ways to be frugal and save money on transportation is to carpool or rideshare. It's also better for the environment and eases road congestion—which helps everyone with their daily commute. Some workplaces have carpool programs and incentives for participating in or leading a rideshare group. Many schools encourage parents to join a carpool or rideshare program because of the influx of cars during drop-off and pick-up times. You can also carpool with friends who work in the same area or with colleagues who have similar schedules. When I've carpooled in the past, I was a passenger, and my contribution was $20 per week for gas. This arrangement also benefited my friend (the driver), because she had an extra $20 per week for fuel, and it wasn't inconvenient since she lived close by and I was already along her route.

- **Plan "circle" trips for errands.** When Hubby and I run errands on the weekend, we make a point of going in a circle to each of the individual stops so that we're not backtracking or using up time and money retracing our steps. Organizing your errands based on where those places are located will allow you to hit everything in one trip. Even arranging your appointments around town on the same day will save you money on gas and car maintenance due to the reduced number of trips—not to mention all of the time you gain by plotting an efficient route in advance. Think about all of the activities and errands you have this weekend outside of the home. Can you organize one trip so that you're not backtracking or retracing your route? It may take a bit of practice, but the more you get into this style of thinking, the more it will become a natural frugal habit.

- **Become a one-car household.** In the U.S., most households have more than one vehicle (9). Often, there's one car for each adult, and sometimes a teenager or older parent has a vehicle as well. Depending on your family's needs, multiple vehicles could make sense, but many frugal families can adapt to using just one. Some manage by arranging schedules so one spouse can drive the other to work. Others coordinate children's extracurricular activities, allowing drop-off and pick-up around the same time for each child. If you're interested in downsizing, start gradually by experimenting with alternate scheduling or public transportation to see if one car could work. Another option is a trial suspension of your car insurance and registration for one month, which forces you to rely on other ways to get around. These exercises can help you determine if your family can make the change without too much sacrifice. Keep in mind that not all frugal families can function with a single vehicle—and that's perfectly fine! If you need more than one car, try using the other tips in this section to reduce your overall transportation costs.

- **Take care of your vehicle.** One of the easiest ways to save money on transportation is also one of the most overlooked: regular vehicle maintenance. By caring for your car and investing a little time and money into upkeep, you can catch small problems before they turn into costly repairs. Regular oil changes (or learning to do them yourself) greatly reduce the risk of engine failure. Interior care matters, too—detailing the cabin and using protective treatments on the dashboard and seats helps prevent wear and cracking. Maintenance also affects resale value, because the better you treat your vehicle now, the more you'll get if you decide to sell it. Simple steps like keeping your tires properly inflated, washing your car regularly, checking fluid levels, and learning basic repairs can go a long way in preserving your investment.

Utilities

As one of your basic needs, utilities are variable expenses that occur regularly throughout the year and fluctuate based on the amount you consume. For example, you may have a high heating bill in the winter due to the cost of keeping your home comfortable despite the cold. In the summer, your water bill could increase with seasonal activities like gardening, lawn maintenance, or filling a child's wading pool on a hot day.

Before you consider ways to save on utilities, take some time to become aware of how much of each utility you and your family consume. This can help you make adjustments to your energy usage behaviours and adopt frugal alternatives. For example, if you wash several loads of laundry each week and use the dryer for every load, you could instead adopt a frugal behaviour by hanging them on a clothesline to dry on warm, sunny days. This will save money on machine drying and also extend the life of your clothing, since line-dried garments tend not to wear out as quickly. You may also discover that items dried in the fresh air have a crisp summer scent, and that you prefer drying linens and towels on a line as well. A frugal hack for fluffy line-dried towels and soft shirts is to place them in the dryer for ten minutes once they've dried outside. This gives you all the benefits of a tumble dryer without much added cost.

Frugal Foundations

- **Turn off lights when you leave the room.** When my grandpa used to come home and find all the lights on, he'd bellow in his best Fred Flintstone impression, "This place is lit up like a Christmas tree!" We'd scatter and giggle as we ran around the house, shutting off lights in rooms that weren't being used. When we were young, we didn't fully understand that turning the lights off when you leave a room is simply practical. There's no need for lights on the other side of the house to be on if no one's there. Yes, there may be times when you want to keep a few lights on—such as for safety reasons or a bit of mood lighting—but for the most part, a simple behaviour change can yield big energy savings.

- **Invest in digital thermostats.** Setting your household temperature at a moderate level is a great way to see reductions in your heating bill. If you don't have one already, consider investing in a digital thermostat that lets you program a set temperature for different times of the day. We set ours to 24°C (75°F) in the summer and 21°C (70°F) in the winter. This means that in summer, our air conditioner only turns on once it's really hot—and during the winter, coming in from sub-zero temperatures outside makes even a moderate interior warmth feel tropical.

- **Bundle up—or down.** I never paid much attention to the crocheted Afghans that were always draped over the back of the couch at Grammy's house—but when my body felt like it needed to warm up, I would unconsciously reach for the blanket instead of the thermostat. The simple act of bundling up inside your home can greatly reduce how much you spend on heating. In the colder months, wear fluffy slippers or thick socks around the house to keep your feet warm. Snuggle up in a housecoat or a comfy cardigan while sitting at your desk or watching TV. Keep throw blankets on your chairs and sofas so everyone can easily get warm without turning up the heat. The reverse concept applies in the summer. Try wearing lightweight, breathable clothing or dressing in layers. Instead of cranking up the air conditioning, change into a tank top and a pair of shorts. At night, switch your duvet or comforter for a thin top sheet to keep cool.

- **Use tap-cold water for laundry.** Many of us were taught that you need to wash clothes in scalding hot water for them to come clean. The reality is quite different: hot water not only sets stains but also has the potential to shrink some of your favourite (and most expensive) clothing items. The cleaning process actually has more to do with the agitation of the clothes in the machine and the power of the detergent than the temperature of the water. By setting your machine to run on the tap-cold setting, you'll not only save money on your heating bill but also on clothing, since cold water preserves colours and doesn't damage individual fibres the way hot water can.

- **Unplug electronics and appliances when not in use.** Most people in North America are surrounded every day by technology and a variety of electronic devices that are constantly plugged in. Even if you aren't actively using an appliance, it's still drawing electricity to stay "at the ready" for the next use. Take a walk around your house and see if any of your appliances are using energy while idle. Anything with a light on is sucking power. You may be thinking, "How much power can a plugged-in toaster use?" But it's not just the toaster—it's the coffee maker, TV, computer, microwave, toaster oven, blender, laundry machines, alarm clocks, video game consoles, and so on. Everything in your home that's currently plugged in uses power. Unplug any items you don't frequently use throughout the day, and plug them in only when necessary to limit passive energy consumption.

- **Use curtains seasonally for shade, heat, and light.** Friends of ours visited recently and mentioned that they weren't sure if we were home because all of the windows were blacked out. In the summer, we save on cooling costs by using blackout curtains to keep the sun from heating up the interior of our home. If we left the curtains wide open and allowed the sun to shine in—particularly in Edmonton, where summer days often reach above 30°C—we'd need a separate income to pay for the air conditioning to keep us cool. The opposite is true in the winter. Since our winters are cold but sunny, we keep the drapes open to allow for a bit of the "greenhouse effect", adding a bit of warmth to our home for free. We also take advantage of the natural sunlight and shut off the lights during the day.

- **Add caulk to windows and draft breaks to doors.** No matter their age, most homes have small gaps around their windows and doors, usually due to the house settling into its foundation. To prevent your money from literally going out the window, try resealing gaps with caulk. Caulk is inexpensive but provides enough of a barrier to keep the warm air in and the cold air out. Check out *How to Caulk a Window* by *Family Handyman* on YouTube for a beginner tutorial (10). Another common leakage location is at the bottom of doors. Draft breaks are long, snake-like sacks usually filled with grain, beans, or poly fibre. They're placed at the bottom of doors leading to the basement, pantry, attic, or garage—areas that aren't usually well-insulated and tend to be cooler. If you're crafty, you can sew your own and create draft breaks for all of your doors.

- **Collect rainwater for gardening.** Water is expensive, and depending on where you live, the climate will dictate how much you need to keep your garden well-hydrated and vibrant. In our area, we regularly get long stretches of extremely hot weather in the summer, which results in large water bills to keep our yard and plants green and lush. Since we put a lot of effort into our garden and don't want to see our crops fail from lack of water, we offset the cost by collecting rainwater. Rainwater is free—other than the expense of the container needed to capture it and keep it protected from insects like mosquitoes (they love standing water for breeding and laying eggs). Rainwater has the added benefit of being natural and free of chemicals like chlorine and fluoride, which are added to tap water. Most buckets attach at the bottom of eavestrough downspouts to collect water whenever it rains.

Social Contact

It may feel like a strange concept to consider ways to save money on your social interactions. But being human often involves participating in social activities that can cost a great deal of money, particularly for large families. As you review your budget, think about how many of your recent expenditures were related to meeting up with friends, going for a meal, attending a club, going out to a movie, or another social event. The cost for a family of four to see a movie, for instance, averages around $100, including tickets, beverages, and snacks—not to mention the cost of gas to get to the theatre and back. Finding creative ways to engage with your social circle frugally can be a fun challenge for you and your family—often leading to the most memorable and rewarding experiences for a fraction of the cost.

Frugal Foundations

- **Be honest about your goals and frugal lifestyle.** When you approach social contact as a new frugarian, be upfront with your friends and family about your lifestyle. Let them know that you're adopting frugal habits and being more conscious about how you're spending your money. Look for opportunities to share that you still want to engage and spend time with them, but that you'd prefer doing things that don't cost much money. If my experience is anything to go by, folks will be grateful to have an alternative to spending a lot of money on going out. This comes back to leading by example. If you put it out there in your social circle that you're frugal, you may be surprised by how many of them will appreciate sharing experiences and connections with the people they care about—without it impacting their bank accounts.

- **Gather for game night.** Bringing friends and family together for a game night is a great way to interact and engage while maintaining your frugal way of life. Game nights are always a good time (ours tend to get a little silly, especially with Pictionary or charades), and you can invite people to bring their favourite games on alternating weeks to keep the selection fresh. You can also suggest that guests bring snacks to share. This will not only provide an affordable entertainment option for all of you, but will also show your social circle that you don't need to spend much money to have fun.

- **Host or join book clubs.** If you enjoy reading, consider joining or hosting a book club for your social group. If you've ever been a part of a book club, the first half hour or so is usually dedicated to talking about the book, and the rest of the time is spent chatting, laughing, and catching up with friends. If you're the host, consider selecting a popular book that's available at the public library so there isn't an upfront cost for others unless they want their own copy. If you're joining someone else's book club, check out the library or thrift store instead of buying the book brand new. Amazon also has a "used book" option for most titles, allowing you to purchase many books second-hand.

- **Potlucks.** As a foodie, some of my favourite frugal events are potlucks. It's not just the delicious variety of dishes to try that makes them so attractive, but the fact that anyone can participate—regardless of their disposable income. When I was starting out in the office many years ago, I looked forward to potlucks as a way to experience different cultures and cuisines. Since I was still a student and low on funds, I would always take my mom's famous Corned Beef Dip—one block of softened cream cheese, one can of corned beef (the one with the cow on it), a small jar of relish, a big squirt of mustard, and lots of black pepper whipped together with a hand mixer, chilled, and served with crackers. It was always a hit, and could still be made today for under $10. Items like coleslaw, veggie sticks and dip, and homemade buns or biscuits can be frugal ways to participate in potlucks.

- **Outdoor activities.** There's a misconception that as soon as you leave the house for an event, you're going to spend money. Obviously, if you're shopping or running errands, your wallet will be lighter when you return home, but that shouldn't be the rule for social outings. As a new frugarian, you can keep costs low by planning events that are activity-based, not consumer-based—having a picnic by an urban pond, playing disc golf, going for a walk in a local park, or planning a playground date with neighbours. You can even plan outdoor events in your own backyard. Whether it's a BBQ with friends and family or pitching a tent for an overnight "camping trip" with your kids, there are many ways to enjoy nature while embracing your frugality.

- **Send letters to friends and family.** In the age of instant communication and invasive availability, the art of letter writing is making a comeback. There's nothing like opening the mailbox and seeing a pretty envelope with your name scrawled across the front—and the immediate joy that comes from knowing someone was thinking of you and cared enough to handwrite a personal message. It shows an intimacy of friendship and camaraderie that can't be conveyed through a cellphone screen or voice message. And remember: if you send out cards and letters to others, they may return the gesture. This is a great way to keep your kids connected with family and friends who live in other parts of the country. You can even try pen-pal exchanges with people in other parts of the world— giving your children a frugal and fun way to learn more about other cultures and form new connections. Explore your local thrift store or ReUse centre for second-hand cards, stationery, and envelopes.

- **Be willing to say no.** As a new frugarian, this might take some getting used to—but it's perfectly acceptable for you to decline if you're invited to an event that doesn't align with your frugality. At one office I worked in, my colleagues would go out for expensive coffees and meals multiple times per week. If I had said "yes" every time I was asked to go, I'd have had no savings in the bank at all. A simple, "No thanks, I usually prefer to bring my own coffee. Maybe another time", will not only set the expectation that you like to bring coffee from home, but it also leaves the invitation open so you can join in when you feel like a treat or want to engage in the social aspect. Trust me, your friends and co-workers won't be offended if you pass, and they may even see the value in bringing their own coffee from home, too—yet another opportunity for you to lead by example!

Education

Learning doesn't have to be expensive or feel like a chore. As a frugarian, I've found that making education part of everyday life is all about setting up an environment that encourages curiosity and makes it easy to explore new skills. With a little planning, you can turn your home into a space that sparks learning—whether it's a bookshelf full of reference materials, a desk with art supplies, or simply knowing where to find free resources online or in your community. Between libraries, thrift stores, second-hand books, and free online courses, there are plenty of frugal ways to challenge yourself and expand your knowledge.

Frugal Foundations

- **Create a learning centre in your home.** Fostering an environment for learning that is engaging and accessible is an essential part of making education both fun and frugal. A learning centre is basically a dedicated space in your home for books, supplies, and materials to help everyone in your household learn and create, such as a desk, paper and pens, or a computer. Our learning centre is in our spare bedroom, which has a bookshelf with an encyclopedia set, a whole bunch of cookbooks, and other fiction and non-fiction titles. In the corner is my crafting station, with a small table and chair, art supplies, and stacks of thrifted magazines to create artisan collages. Each person in your household can have a personal book collection in their room, but by keeping a centralized collection of educational items available to everyone, it becomes a way to connect and share ideas about what you're learning and creating from those materials.

- **Get library cards.** For frugarians, library cards open up a world of free education. Whether you want to explore new recipes, pick up another language, or learn how to maintain your car, the public library is an excellent resource. Many libraries also offer free courses and tutorials for skills like internet basics or introduction to writing. Library cards often provide access to digital resources such as audiobooks, podcasts, and webinars. Our municipal library card even gives us access to LinkedIn Learning, which has short eCourses and learning paths on a variety of business, technology, and career topics. Make sure to keep track of when you check out library items and return them on time, so you can avoid late fees.

- **Buy reference and lesson books at thrift stores.** If you're looking to build a learning library, check the "Education" section of your local thrift store. At the end of each semester, textbooks and reference materials often show up by the boxload. From marketing and economics to English and biology, there are books on virtually any topic of interest. A few years ago, I found a book about insects in the children's section, and it's now one of my favourites. I also grabbed a "Dummies" book on investing for Canadians. Most thrift stores carry lesson books for children as well, often separated by age group—a great addition to any home's learning centre.

- **Explore Massive Open Online Courses (MOOCs).** Advancements in digital technology have made it possible to connect remotely to courses from anywhere in the world, and MOOCs have flourished as a result. These free online courses are offered by international universities (e.g., Harvard, Oxford, UCLA) to give students from diverse backgrounds the chance to learn skills that can improve their quality of life. I've used MOOCs numerous times, mainly to get better at Excel and learn more about computers. Some institutions also offer learning paths that can lead to accredited certification for a reduced tuition fee. Check out edX, Coursera, and Alison to explore courses that interest you.

- **Buy school supplies second-hand.** Back-to-school can be an expensive time of year, and the cost of supplies can put a dent in your budget. By keeping an eye out for items at garage sales, thrift stores, and eco-stations, you can start building a stash of supplies for any student in your household. One of my favourite places for second-hand school supplies is the ReUse centre, where they charge $5 for 50 pounds of goods. I go there for scrap paper, magazines, crayons, pencil crayons, cardboard, binders, lined paper, paper clips, staples, desk organizers, and folders. If you have children in different age groups, save unused or lightly-worn supplies at the end of each school year so they can be shared and used again in September. This is even easier if you avoid trends and stick to basic binders, notebooks, and pens in primary colours instead of trendy character prints or patterns—which are usually much more expensive, too.

- **Use the computers and printers at school.** When I was in university, I was the typical broke student. I couldn't afford my own computer or printer, but my school had multiple libraries and computer labs where students could work on assignments, save their work, and print the finished products. Most schools have several computers in the library and classrooms available for students to use for free. Instead of buying your own computer, mouse, keyboard, monitors, cables, printer, ink, and paper, consider using the public access computers and printing stations at your school or local library.

- **Pick a state or provincial school.** Many of us automatically think of elite Ivy League schools or private universities when we imagine the college experience. Somehow, we've bought into the idea that the only good education is an expensive one, and that the only way to get a decent job is with a degree from a prestigious private university. While education is important, it's essential to consider the long-term impact of hundreds of thousands of dollars in debt. One way to reduce that burden is to attend a state or provincial college. Studying locally is one of the most cost-effective and frugal ways to cut tuition. Private or out-of-state universities can cost an estimated 3.5 times more than public ones (11). Over a 4-year undergraduate degree, that's the difference between $40,000 and $140,000. Another frugal option is to attend community college for the first two years and then transfer to a university. This can save a lot on tuition and also ease students into both the college experience and adulthood.

Pen-and-Paper Budget

You don't need fancy software or a computer spreadsheet to create an effective budget. A simple coil-bound notebook is all you need to draft a pen-and-paper budget. At the top of the page, write the month. Divide the page into thirds from top to bottom. Label the first column "Monthly Income/Balance," the second column "Expenses," and the third column "Cost" (see the Simple Budget table below).

As you prepare to start plotting your budget, consider the following:

- What did your spending look like over the past three months?
- Were the basic needs of you and your family covered?
- Were you more often over- or under-budget?
- If you were under budget, what did you do with your surplus at the end of each month?
- If you were over budget, how much were you over? What is the interest rate on that debt?
- How much of your budget was dedicated to debt repayment?
- How much of your budget was set aside as savings?
- How much of your budget was dedicated to charitable giving?
- Are you committed to setting a budget and sticking to it?

Simple Budgeting

The table below shows a simple sample budget based on $4,000 net monthly income for an average family of four:

Monthly Income/Balance	Expenses	Cost
$4,000	Rent/Mortgage	$1,500
$2,500	Groceries	$800
$1,700	Household Items/Pet Food	$100
$1,600	Utilities	$75
$1,525	Home Insurance	$50
$1,475	Medical Insurance	$250
$1,225	Car Payment/Insurance	$500
$725	Gas/Transportation	$200
$525	Cable/Internet	$75
$450	Phone	$100
$350	Bank Fees	$15
$335	Debt Repayment	$100
$235	Cash Savings	$50
$185	Long-term Savings	$25
$160	Emergency Fund	$25
$135	Clothing and Gifts	$100
$35	Charitable Giving	$25
$10	Surplus	$10
0		

The goal of each month is to budget so your balance is zero and to endeavour to stay on budget, even if it means borrowing from other areas—such as driving less and walking more during the last week of the month to afford essentials.

Your budget is unique and depends on your individual situation and goals—which also means you'll have your own approach to keeping it balanced. The most important consideration in budget planning is ensuring that all of the basic needs of you and your family are covered.

If you don't have enough funds in your "Income" column to cover your monthly expenses, you have a few options:

- **Spend less money in one area to cover expenses in another.** For example, if your family has both cable television and internet, consider cancelling the cable and switching to free options, such as borrowing DVDs from the library or using its free streaming access, or watching free video content at home on platforms like YouTube or Tubi.

- **Take on a side hustle.** Earn extra money, supplement your income, and pay down debt with a casual part-time gig. Popular side hustles for frugarians include yard work and snow shovelling, handyman maintenance, arts and crafts, delivery driving, part-time retail, and pet or house sitting.

- **Consider a different job.** A longer-term goal is to look for a different job or career path with better earning potential and advancement opportunities. While this may require additional training or certification, many learning resources are available free online or through the public library. Work experience opportunities in new-to-you fields are often available through volunteering or internships.

If you look at the sample budget, there are a number of opportunities to reduce and streamline costs—especially since there is money allotted for savings and charitable giving. These categories should be left off the budget if there aren't enough funds to cover your basic expenses. Once you can afford it, you should always strive to budget for your emergency fund and long-term savings. Even if all you can afford is $5 per month in each category, it's an important step in starting the habit of "paying yourself first". It's a small sacrifice to ensure that a portion of your monthly pay is automatically squirrelled away for a rainy day.

Month-Forward Budgeting

One of my favourite frugal strategies to safeguard against unexpected events, such as a job loss or medical expense, is to plan your budget based on what you'll need for the following month. Essentially, you're always prepared and funded for expenses one month in advance. New frugarians who already have savings can implement this plan right away. Those who are operating more on a month-to-month basis can make "month-forward" budgeting one of their early financial goals. The dollar amount of this savings goal would be equivalent to one month's take-home pay (net income) for each family member who contributes funds toward expenses.

Pay-Period Budgeting

If you're one of the many people who get paid biweekly instead of twice per month, you're fortunate to have 26 pay periods each year instead of the typical 24. "Pay-period" budgeting is all about running your budget on a fixed monthly amount equivalent to two pay periods. This means that twice per year, you get a "free paycheque". You obviously still earned the money, but since you're operating on a budget of two paycheques per month, those additional pay periods are a bonus above and beyond what you've allocated for income. This can be a great way to accelerate your financial goals. I usually use a portion of those funds to make larger charitable donations, purchase something from my "want" list, or increase our cash savings and pantry stockpile.

The Envelope System

This simple, cash-based budgeting method uses an envelope pouch with individual slots to divide your net income into different categories. Those slots can be used to separate your income by week, by expense type—such as groceries or transportation—or by specific savings goals like a vacation or a major home repair. In my envelope system, I have enough slots to separate out my major expenses by each week in the month. If I go under budget one week on groceries, for instance, I move the money forward to the next week's grocery slot so I can spend it that week on more ingredients, higher-quality items, or dry goods and pantry staples to build out my stockpile. At the end of the month, any surplus cash I have gets divided equally between long-term savings, cash savings, stockpile, investments, and charitable giving. This efficient cycle of spending, sharing, and saving continues month over month as long as you stick to your budget. Pouches can be purchased at most dollar stores, but you can also make your own using a large envelope with several smaller envelopes inside.

Financial Consistency

Being on top of your income and expenditures is integral to leading a frugal lifestyle. Staying consistent in your approach to budgeting and saving will help you achieve your financial goals more effectively, while also ensuring the basic needs of you and your family are routinely met. After putting in the effort to create your initial budget, you might try it for a few months and then toss it aside, thinking you have it all figured out (or you don't want to worry about it). But just as practicing scales and performing in front of a crowd are key to being a successful musician, consistently following a budget is the foundation and mainstay of your frugality.

Create a Budget and Stick to It

To successfully live within your means as a frugarian, you need to create a monthly budget and strive as much as possible to stick to it. If you consistently have difficulty staying on budget, try looking back at previous months to track your spending. Most banks have trackers on their online statements that show what category your expenses fall into (restaurants, entertainment, sporting events, grocery stores, etc.). This can be an effective way to see how your money is being spent each month—and also help you adjust your budget to ensure you're not falling short or dipping into overdraft or credit card debt.

Live Within Your Means

These days, living within your means seems like a foreign concept to many people, and the "charge-it" mentality is in full force. Since the early 1970s, society has been obsessed with credit and the instant gratification that comes from buying now and paying later. Rarely in history has the credit bubble been so inflated, with individual incomes leveraged so heavily into the red. By the second quarter of 2025, the debt-to-income ratio had climbed to 174.9%, meaning Canadians owed $1.75 for every dollar of disposable income (12). During the same period, the average American household carried approximately $152,653 in debt (13). Instead of working, earning, saving, and waiting to purchase something they need or that has value, many people give in to impulse and buy whatever they want—regardless of whether they can afford it.

Unfortunately, the ease and accessibility of online shopping have made this problem even worse. The thrill of a purchase is fleeting, and we enjoy a false sense of satisfaction from buying something we wanted immediately, simply because we wanted it. It's not until the credit card bill arrives at the end of the month—often with interest rates well in excess of 20%—that the glow of that purchase begins to dim and the chains of debt are felt again. But by making strides each month to live within your means, you can avoid falling into debt altogether. And if you already have debt, your budget can help you set out a plan to pay it off as quickly as possible.

Set Savings Goals

Naturally, everyone's individual targets will be different, but setting savings goals can help keep you on track and prevent you from going over budget. Specific goals may also motivate you to consistently set aside funds for occasions, activities, and items you want, instead of taking on debt because you have no surplus. It also makes the small sacrifices easier to bear when you have clear goals set out before you— and you're working each day toward them.

One of our main financial goals is to purchase a house. We want to make a substantial down payment (at least 20%), so we currently rent a modest bungalow for much less than it would cost to carry a mortgage with only a 5% down payment. The money we save by renting is put into our "House Fund", which is steadily (yet modestly) growing each month.

Patience is another big part of goal setting, particularly if you're currently in debt. It may feel like you'll be in debt forever, with no way out. But by making small, incremental changes and adjusting your spending and earning behaviours, your needs-based financial goals will become easier to achieve.

Budget for Wants

On the surface, budgets may seem rigid and unyielding to occasional indulgences. However, while frugarian budgets tend to limit those types of expenditures, they certainly don't eliminate them. As you create your budget, it's important to be realistic and allocate some of your surplus income for things that would be considered "wants". If you're in debt, that amount should be quite low (if funded at all) until you've paid off what you owe. As a frugarian, the portion of surplus you set aside for your wants should be on the lower side—and when you shop, you should still look for deals and sales to maximize how far those funds will stretch.

For higher-priced items, set a goal to purchase them within a specific timeframe. Then, take a portion of your "wants" budget and set it aside for that item until you've reached your goal. It may require a behaviour change, but it's much more mentally freeing to set aside $25 per month for future wants than to pay $25 in credit card interest.

A few years ago, I wanted an alternative to taking the bus around town on weekends. Setting aside $50 per month from my budget surplus allowed me to buy an urban kick-scooter within about six months. Not only that, but because I worked hard to save for it—and it was something I truly wanted—the sacrifice and patience made the reward feel like a worthwhile achievement.

Charitable Giving

One of the greatest benefits of leading a frugal lifestyle is the ability to donate a portion of your net income to charity. For some frugarians, charitable giving takes the form of contributions to their faith community—for others, it means donating to a homeless shelter or local food bank. However you choose to give back, take a moment to reflect on your initial motivations for adopting a frugal lifestyle. Consider how your focus on meeting your family's basic needs can also enable you to help those who are struggling to meet their own.

Frugal Foundations

- **Charitable commitment.** Deciding to donate to charity can be an uplifting and emotional experience. During a difficult time in my early twenties, I relied on our neighbourhood food bank for several weeks, picking up bags filled with groceries and personal hygiene products. It wasn't much, but it was enough to help me meet a major need when I couldn't do so myself. Many frugarians share the goal of charitable giving. By committing to donate even a small amount each month, you can help support the well-being of others. One simple way to ease into giving is to buy one extra pantry staple, such as a can of beans or boxed pasta, when you're shopping and place it in the food bank bin.

- **Donate what you can afford.** The beauty of charitable giving is that there's no set dollar amount required. Some people with higher incomes can afford to give hundreds each month, while others may contribute a few dollars. Whatever the amount, it's important to give only what you can afford and never go into debt to do so.

- **Donate time, not money.** When you and your family are considering ways to give back, remember that generosity doesn't always require spending money. Volunteering your time and energy is a wonderful way to combine charitable giving with your frugal lifestyle. You may visit seniors as a companion, help local children learn to read, sort food at your community food bank, or prepare and serve meals at a soup kitchen. Whatever your budget, consider donating your time as one of your financial goals.

Part 6
Frugal Family

Transitioning to a frugal lifestyle can be a challenge for families—especially when children are involved. It can feel strange for kids raised by non-frugal parents to adopt a frugal lifestyle. Most often, they've grown accustomed to their parents' spending habits, which can be tough to break—especially when the outcome is pleasurable, as buying new things often is.

Children of all ages are impressionable. They're influenced by family, peers, advertisements, and social norms. By easing your kids into the frugal lifestyle, you can help them learn the value of money and set them on the path toward their own frugal future. Having your children on board during your family's transition will make it easier for everyone to adopt a frugal lifestyle day-to-day, because you're working together toward a common goal.

Preschool (0 to 5 Years)

As early as three years old, I remember waking up to the smell of my mom's homemade bread. I was allowed to help out in the kitchen at that age and learned simple recipes early on. I didn't realize until much later in life that my mom was teaching me the skills I would need to lead a frugal lifestyle as an adult. Subconsciously, I was absorbing that knowledge and filing it away in my mental "toolkit" for later use.

Today, it's trendy to batch cook and meal prep, but these practices have been the norm in frugal households for generations. Back in my preschool years, I would watch my mom pack homemade lunches for my dad and sister and cook hearty prairie meals like pot roast and spare ribs to last for several meals during the week. I didn't realize it at the time, but by living frugally every day and passing down the knowledge she had learned from her own mother and grandmother, my mom was planting the seed of frugality within me. The transition to a frugal lifestyle is often easiest for children under five, who follow their parents' lead and have little need for decision-making at that point in their lives.

Frugal Foundations

- **Lead by example.** Share your frugal habits with your young children and encourage them to engage and ask questions about why you've adopted certain frugal behaviours.
- **Normalize it.** "Going frugal" doesn't need to be a big event. Making modest changes and transitioning at your own pace can make the move to frugality easier for kids.
- **Let kids help in the kitchen.** When you're preparing meals—especially if you're cooking from scratch—bring your children into the kitchen and show them how tools and appliances are used and how recipes come together. They'll learn that cooking is easy and that delicious food can be simple and homemade.
- **Gift from the heart.** Preschool is a great age to start teaching your kids about handcrafted gifts made with love. Get your kids crafting by upcycling old greeting cards and construction paper into adorable cards and personalized art projects to give to others. By teaching children at an early age that gifts don't need to cost much money, you'll set realistic (and affordable) expectations for future holidays and occasions—and show them that the most cherished gifts are often those made with our hands and given with our hearts.

Grade School (5 to 13 Years)

Elementary school-aged kids are usually easygoing when transitioning to the frugal lifestyle. However, due to the influence of advertising and peer pressure from other children, it's not without its challenges for parents. Grade school age is when kids become ensnared in the "toys" culture. The incessant advertising directed at children can leave them feeling left out if they don't possess the same "wants" as their friends. At this age, frugal parents should strive to maintain a balance between frugality and social acceptance. There is little that impacts grade school children more than bullying—and nothing incites bullying more than the perception of being different.

During my childhood, my mom did her best to strike a balance between maintaining our frugal lifestyle and making sure I wasn't a social outcast. We shopped sales and clearance racks for clothing that was on-brand but discounted. We hosted sleepovers with friends that cost very little for us out of pocket. My sister and I were also encouraged to spend time outside, exploring our neighbourhood and enjoying nature. I first learned how the library worked in grade school and became a certified "bookworm". I even joined reading clubs and book swaps with other kids who also preferred reading as their main hobby.

It was during grade school that I started to shop for clothing at thrift stores with my mom. I always looked at it as a fun challenge to try to find cute clothes in the bargain bin. Although I was rarely trendy, I had the clothes I needed and developed a traditional, preppy style that I still wear today. Since those fashions never really go out of style, I was able to wear the same clothing for multiple seasons just by adding other accessories or styling my hair in different ways.

For many frugal families, grade school is when they start giving their children a weekly allowance. This small amount of regular "income" can help kids start to learn the value of money, how to differentiate between wants and needs, and how to save their pennies to purchase wants of their own. How much you choose to give each child per week is up to you. A common amount is $1 per year of age per week (e.g., $10 per week for a 10-year-old).

Keep in mind that not all families give out allowances, particularly when funds are tight. A non-monetary option for allowance is to have a basket of "coupons" that each child can pick from each week. You're at the whim of your creativity when deciding what coupons to create. Some options include extra TV time, a sleepover, homemade pizza night, or a trip to a community playground. When each child makes their selection, that is their special "allowance" for the week. This also helps teach children that you don't need a lot of money to have a fun and fulfilling life.

While I did receive occasional pocket money, I didn't receive a regular allowance in grade school. Instead, I took a course to become a certified babysitter. The community-delivered training taught me basic first aid, home economics, and infant hygiene. After acquiring a few regular customers, I was able to start building my savings. In fifth and sixth grades, I set a small financial goal to save up for a trip to Disneyland. The deal was that if I could cover my airfare, my mom would pay for the rest of the trip. I babysat when I had free time for nearly two years. At the end of it, I got to have an amazing trip and memories to last a lifetime—all because of a few frugal habits and a little hustle.

This was also the age when I got my first savings account. It was an account designed just for kids and didn't have an annual fee. It came with a little money-tracking booklet to write down my running balance and all of the expenses that came out of the account. Seeing how quickly my $20 babysitting loot would dwindle after making impulse purchases (like smelly stickers, colourful erasers, and various New Kids on the Block swag) helped me to learn simple budgeting. I quickly understood that if I bought something for one amount, I would have only so much leftover. It was also during this time that I learned to do without wants when we simply couldn't afford them—and to be grateful for everything I had.

Frugal Foundations

- **Understand peer pressure.** Elementary school can be a difficult age for children. What may seem frivolous to adults could be socially essential for kids. Hosting parties, movie nights, or play dates are frugal ways to help your kids interact within their social groups.

- **Stick to a classic style.** By choosing to dress your kids in more traditional clothes like simple t-shirts and pants, you're laying the groundwork to avoid the pitfalls (and expense) of brand marketing. A non-branded hoodie, shirt, pants, and runners can look just as nice as their designer counterparts. Even choosing basic duffle bags and backpacks can save a lot of money without sacrificing quality or function.

- **Learn the library together.** The library can be a great way to provide access to a variety of fun "wants" without spending any money. Going to the library can also be an activity that involves other children in their social group, whether through reading circles, book clubs, or themed activity days.

- **Start giving allowance.** Set aside a small portion of your monthly budget for allowances. Base your allowances on what you can afford, but aim to spend no more than $1 per year of age, per child, per week. Consider frugal allowance options like "coupons", where they can invite a friend over for a movie, freshly popped popcorn, and homemade hot chocolate—or any number of other creative activities and snacks suited to their personalities and preferences.

- **Start a savings account.** A kid-friendly savings account can be a great way to help children learn the responsibilities of money, the value of doing chores around the house to earn a small "income", and how to budget for items they want. Many banks will allow you to set up a children's savings account for free if their parent is an account holder.

- **Set up small financial goals.** All kids want *stuff*, but that doesn't mean you have to buy them everything they want. Setting small financial goals can help children see the value of hard work and help them learn patience to save money effectively long term. Realistic and achievable financial goals can also help kids learn to avoid the traps of instant gratification. You can help them set goals for things like a video game system, a special family trip, or an adventure to a recreation centre or amusement park.

- **Consider a kid-friendly side hustle.** Check your community bulletin board for youth opportunities and let your friends and family know your kids are available for hire! Suitable jobs for kids include setting up a lemonade stand, delivering retail flyers or newspapers, babysitting, raking leaves, shovelling snow, or dog walking. To help them achieve their savings goals, have your children set aside a portion of their money earned to put into their savings account or piggy bank—50% is a good benchmark for savings since it mirrors future tax and benefit obligations.

- **Involve them in frugal tasks.** Elementary-aged kids are often eager to help out with things like hanging the wash on the line or rearranging the cans of stockpiled goods after a shopping trip. Involving your children in your frugal habits will help them see frugality as a normal part of daily life. For older children, it's a great age to introduce them to the family budget. Showing them how you allocate your monthly income into different categories can help them see the value of a dollar and how quickly expenses can add up. Try to engage them in light budget planning with your grocery budget. Give them a set dollar amount and see how they would make it stretch to meet your family's food needs for that week.

High School (14 to 18)

Teenaged children sometimes face challenges transitioning to the frugal lifestyle, and it's not just the result of stubbornness and independence at that age. It's because no other age group faces the stress of conformity and the burdens of peer pressure like kids in high school. Fitting in often involves wearing trendy clothes, eating out, shopping, going to movies, and doing any number of social activities that involve spending money.

Anyone who has been through high school understands the gross emphasis placed on belonging. Teens try to impress each other by showing off their "stuff" to other kids and displaying their parents' wealth (or debt). In a world where social media and influencers are cultural norms, there's a perception and expectation among many youths that life isn't worth living unless you wear certain brands, own certain items, or engage in certain expensive activities. As a frugarian, you can help ease your teenage children into the frugal lifestyle by leading by example and involving them in your frugal behaviours. Activities like thrift store shopping for clothing, accessories, and bedroom décor can help them learn frugal skills that will not only help them transition into frugality but also adulthood.

High school is also an ideal time for your teen to start working a part-time job with more responsibility than just delivering the daily paper. Part-time employment is often among the most fun and rewarding times in a teen's life—and a great way to teach financial accountability. Working part time exposes teens to what it's really like to be employed, to have a boss, to have responsibilities, to be paid for completing the duties required of their role, and to pay income taxes. They'll receive regular paycheques, make deposits into their savings account, and take out a portion for their expenses. These skills will help them build a strong frugal foundation for their future.

Frugality was already second nature to me by the time I reached high school. Still, I was encouraged to take courses that aligned with my frugal lifestyle. In Career and Life Management class, I gained life skills like how to write a resume and prepare for an interview. I also learned about credit, interest, and how to create (and stick to) a monthly budget. In Home Economics, I was trained on the basics of cooking, how to budget for groceries, and how to create tasty meals out of simple, inexpensive ingredients.

Adolescence as a frugarian was pretty easy in the 1990s because it was the Grunge era and a resurgence of Sixties style was in full swing. Instead of buying designer clothes at the mall, my friends and I went thrift store shopping and scoured the racks for the cheapest and most stylish outfits. Not only did we end up with on-trend, inexpensive clothes, but we also treated thrifting as a social activity that anyone in our peer group could enjoy, regardless of how much money they had to spend.

Frugal Foundations

- **Lead by example.** Children of any age are impressionable and guided by the actions of their parents. Seeing how you live frugally day to day will help them understand that they can lead fulfilling lives without overextending themselves financially.
- **Share your frugal knowledge.** By taking opportunities to teach your teens frugal habits, you'll help them transition out of high

school. You can set them up for success by involving them in activities like meal planning, budgeting, and grocery shopping while encouraging them to help out in the kitchen.

- **Teach them to cook.** One of the most valuable pieces of frugal knowledge you can share with your teens is to teach them how to cook. You don't have to be Gordon Ramsay to show them the basics of cooking a couple of egg dishes, pancakes, a simple spaghetti and meatballs, or something more advanced like a roasted chicken with mashed potatoes. As they move into their college years, your kids will be grateful for any cooking tips you can give them to make simple, healthy meals in an apartment or dormitory kitchen.

- **Support them in working part-time.** If their school and family schedule permits, encourage your teen to take on a part-time job. Not only will this help them learn employment skills, but it will also show them firsthand how much effort it takes to earn money. To keep it frugal, work with your teen to find a job close to home so they can walk, bike, or take public transit.

College (18 to 22)

College-aged kids (even if they no longer live at home) can benefit greatly from transitioning to a frugal lifestyle. As a frugarian, you can guide them to make frugal adjustments to their spending habits as they become more independent and self-sufficient. Remember, most college kids are on tight budgets. The more you can teach them now, the less they will have to learn the hard way. This is also an excellent time to warn them about debt and credit cards and the importance of focusing the majority of their money on the items they actually need.

When I went off to college in the fall after high school, I felt well-equipped to take on my new role as an adult because I had already worked part-time, understood how a chequing account and interest worked, and spent a few weeks before school working on my semester budget. That's not to say that I was perfect at managing my money—I enjoyed plenty of pizza and beer like most college kids, and had a bad experience with my first credit card. However, I strived to avoid overextending myself, even if it meant skipping the more expensive activities like bars, restaurants, or sporting events.

During my second year of college, I realized that I had enough time to take on a part-time job. I picked up about 15 hours per week working at a clothing store in the local shopping centre. This job gave me additional work experience to put on my resume and lessened my overall student loan debt.

Frugal Foundations

- **Support self-sufficiency.** For most teens, college is the first time they're fully responsible for managing their own income and expenses. Support their self-sufficiency by offering advice while also allowing them to figure some things out on their own. This will give them enough independence to learn from their experiences while gaining confidence in their abilities to lead a financially responsible adult life.

- **Help with their first-term budget.** For many students, their student loan or educational savings account is the first time they gain access to a large amount of money. From personal experience, I can tell you it can be overwhelming, especially if you didn't grow up with money. Seeing a $25,000 balance in my account on the first day of school honestly felt like I won the lottery. Without proper planning and a thorough budget that allows for fun and entertainment, your student may find that they get to the end of the money before they reach the end of the term. Working with your child through their first-term budget will also help you both see potential shortcomings. It's a chance to discuss options for how to make up the difference, such as a stipend from you or a part-time job for them.

- **Caution about debt and credit cards.** Visit any college campus today, and you'll find kiosks from major banks promising your child the world if they would just sign up for a high-interest credit card. The attraction to buy now/pay later is often too much to resist, and many students fall into the trap of multiple credit cards, maxed-out limits, and high monthly payments. This can be devastating for teens who are just learning to manage their money. This early misstep can trap them in a debt/ minimum payment hole that can take years to crawl out of.

- **Don't be quick to bail them out.** Part of teaching your college-aged kids about money and the freedom of frugality is allowing them to make mistakes. Too often, parents are quick to jump to their child's rescue when they stumble financially. Unless the error is so large that it would cause significant harm to their credit score, let them make the little financial foibles that will teach them lasting lessons in budgeting, spending, and saving.

Part 7
Frugal Food

Food is the only major need that I'm dedicating a whole section of this book to. Not only does food have unlimited frugal potential, but it's also the area that can see the greatest gains by investing time and effort, not just money. The sad reality is that food is a necessity that many people struggle to afford. Food availability and "food deserts" are impacting families across North America, and many people are struggling to put food on the table. In other cases, some people overspend on addictive and convenient fast food and processed junk—I've been one of them, and there were even times in college when I went into debt to satisfy cravings and social outings that I couldn't afford. Others have not yet learned the cooking skills that made food prep and seasonal preservation part of our parents' and grandparents' daily routines.

Food is the family's lifeblood and a way to connect, share, grow, and learn. By approaching your family's food in a frugal way, you have the opportunity to prepare more healthy, home-cooked meals and teach your children the value of what they eat—where it comes from, how to store it, and how to prepare it. You'll show them that frugal, modest meals can be wholesome and delicious and that special occasions in the comfort of your home can be just as enjoyable as fancy restaurant meals. As you gain confidence in your cooking and budgeting skills, feeding your family with a frugal mindset will become the perfect recipe for money savings, food security, and nutrition.

Frugal Foodie

It's natural to think that if food is frugal, it will be plain, boring, and lacking flavour. However, since your new frugal lifestyle will focus on humble home cooking, you should strive to get creative with your meals and embrace diverse cuisines and cooking methods. By becoming a frugal foodie, you'll be able to create delicious dishes based on good deals and less expensive ingredients—and use herbs and vegetables grown in your garden to supplement your food budget. Hubby and I are die-hard foodies. We cook delicious, satisfying meals because it makes it much easier to avoid the temptation of eating out or ordering takeout—and honestly, our food is better than most menu items we would order from a restaurant. Practice makes perfect, and cooking skills are quickly learned with a little bit of trial and error.

Frugal Foundations

- **Try new recipes.** The easiest way to hone your skills and become a frugal foodie is to be adventurous and experiment with new recipes. With resources like the library, the Food Network, and YouTube, anyone can develop the skills needed to become a confident home cook. If you have a favourite cuisine or a dish you've always wanted to master, experimenting is a great way to flex your muscles and grow as a great home cook. By looking for ways to replicate restaurant-style dishes, you'll also be less inclined to eat out.

- **Maximize flavour with fresh herbs and spices.** One of the most frugal ways to stretch your food dollar is to use less expensive ingredients enhanced with aromatics. Investing in your herbs and spices cupboard can pay dividends in increased flavour—and once they're in your arsenal, you only need a small amount to make a significant impact on taste. To start building out your stockpile, pick up one new bottle each time you buy groceries. A popular choice for frugarians is to buy herbs and spices from the bulk bins—it's much less expensive than buying individual bottles because you're not paying for the packaging. Look for mix-and-match spice jars at thrift stores and garage sales.

- **Join Pinterest.** One of my favourite activities is to make Pinterest boards of recipes I want to try later. All of the high-quality photographs of delicious, mouth-watering food are enough to make anyone want to try the recipes for themselves. On my Pinterest, I have recipe boards for each meal of the day, as well as snacks and desserts. I also pin recipes for specific types of food, like Italian, Chinese, or Mexican, and have even created diet-specific boards for recipes that align with my current health and fitness goals. Since Pinterest boards are public, you can also share your favourite recipe collections for other people to enjoy.

Home Cooking

A friend recently asked me: "What does frugality mean to you?" I responded simply by saying, "Living within your means and making do with what you have". But when I dug deeper and thought about the heart of frugality, everything came back to home cooking. As a new frugarian, home cooking is an ideal way to save money and ease your family into the frugal lifestyle. It's also an insurance policy on poor health because you'll naturally be eating more nutritious food if you cook the majority of your meals from scratch.

As you approach home cooking as a frugarian, consider the types of food you currently cook at home and those you tend to take out or order at restaurants. Your challenge will be to begin recreating those meals as frugally as you can while achieving the same delicious flavours and textures you crave from restaurant food. You may be a seasoned foodie, or you may be transitioning to home cooking from a place of fast food, TV dinners, and delivery. No matter your skill level, it's essential to start with the basic skills and simple, traditional recipes. If you embrace home cooking with a curious spirit, your stomach and creativity will guide you. Look to friends and family for their favourite simple recipes, too! If a friend makes the most delicious warm spinach dip you've ever tasted, seek them out for the recipe and how they made it. Recipe swapping is a great way to spread knowledge and encourage others to embrace home cooking.

Frugal Foundations

- **Eat at home as much as possible.** By cooking most of your meals at home, you'll naturally prepare more food from scratch (or mostly from scratch). This gives you plenty of chances to try new recipes and quickly hone your kitchen skills. Cooking your own meals not only offers nutritional benefits, but also allows you to save money—funds that can be spent on quality ingredients and kitchen tools to round out your essential equipment.

- **Simplify snacking.** Preparing simple homemade snacks like granola bars, cookies, apple slices, or cut-up vegetables will make it less necessary for you to purchase ready-made snacks at the store. As you cook more of your meals from scratch, you may also discover that you snack less throughout the day. Natural foods are more nutritious and often contain more fibre than their processed or fast-food counterparts—keeping you satiated for longer.

- **Master the basics.** You don't have to be Ina Garten or Jamie Oliver to become an effective home cook. By mastering the simplest version of basic recipes, you can equip yourself with the fundamental skills you need to either cook your meals completely from scratch or make home-cooked meals with the help of pantry staples like pasta sauce, canned turkey, and corn tortillas.

- **Embrace mistakes as learning.** We all make mistakes in the kitchen, and there's nothing you can do but throw it in the garbage and try again. Experimenting is one of the best parts of cooking, but those experiments don't always go to plan. As a frugarian, it can be tough to see food go to waste, but sometimes it's part of the learning process. When I was in culinary school, I accidentally made a massive batch of sweet dough with cups and cups of salt instead of sugar—25 pounds of dough had to be thrown out. But I learned from that mistake, and to this day, I always taste salt and sugar before adding them to a recipe.

I recommend heading to the library or visiting YouTube to check out the following basic home cooking recipes and techniques:

- Stock (beef, chicken, fish, vegetable, mushroom)
- Oatmeal (with rolled and old-fashioned oats)
- Porridge (with Cream of Wheat, Sunny Boy, farro, bulgur, etc.)
- Grits
- Eggs (fried, scrambled, boiled, poached, etc.)
- Potatoes (mashed, roasted, hashbrowns, rösti, au gratin, scalloped, etc.)
- Pancakes (classic, buttermilk, chocolate chip, blueberry, buckwheat, oat, etc.)
- French toast
- One-bowl muffins (blueberry, apple cinnamon, orange cranberry, chocolate, lemon poppyseed, carrot, etc.)
- Grilled cheese sandwiches

- Simple soup (chicken noodle, beef and barley, potato cheddar, spiced butternut squash, carrot and ginger, bean and bacon, cream of mushroom, clam chowder, minestrone, etc.)
- Chili (classic, beef, vegetarian, etc.)
- Perfectly cooked pasta
- Tomato pasta sauce (marinara, bolognese, ragu, classic spaghetti sauce, etc.)
- Alfredo sauce
- Béchamel sauce (creamy white sauce)
- Rice (white, brown, long-grain, arborio, sticky, etc.)
- Roasted chicken and turkey
- Roasted beef, pork, and lamb
- Pot roast (beef, pork, and lamb)
- Stew (vegetarian, beef, pork, and lamb)
- Oven-baked ribs
- Meatballs
- Hamburgers
- Pan gravy
- Cooked dried beans (pinto, black, chickpeas, cannellini, navy, kidney, red, etc.)
- Cooked lentils (red, yellow, green, split peas, etc.)
- Steamed, sautéed, braised, and roasted vegetables
- Rice pudding and tapioca
- Easy no-knead bread
- Easy no-knead dinner buns
- Biscuits
- Flour tortillas
- Pie dough
- Cornbread

- Fresh pasta
- One-bowl cookies (chocolate chip, oatmeal raisin, peanut butter, shortbread, thumbprint, gingerbread, ginger snaps, etc.)
- Brownies
- Basic cake (white, chocolate, spiced, carrot, red velvet, etc.)
- Buttercream and icing
- Seasoned salt
- Mixed herb seasoning
- Cajun seasoning
- Compound butter
- Teriyaki sauce
- Sweet-and-sour sauce
- BBQ sauce
- Table syrup
- One-pot meals
- Five-ingredient meals
- Sheet pan dinners

Once you master a few of the basics, you'll gain confidence to explore different recipes and try new cooking techniques. Have fun with it and remember—you can take learning at your own pace. Start with the more basic recipes on this list and build up to more complex recipes, more challenging cooking methods, and more distinct international cuisine.

Frugal Kitchen

Setting up your frugal kitchen is one of the most important steps you'll take in your new frugal journey. The kitchen is the heartbeat of the home, and by having it accessible, easy-to-use, and convenient for food storage and preparation, you're setting yourself up for frugal success. In a frugal household, the kitchen is where the magic happens. With proper kitchen tools and ingredients, you can transform plain flour into delicious bread. You can turn fresh eggs into a delicious omelet or frittata. You can turn the humble potato into a versatile and nutritious staple for any daily meal.

Setting up your kitchen doesn't have to break the bank. Check out Kijiji, thrift stores, garage sales, and the clearance section of your local retailers for any items you need to make your kitchen a place you enjoy cooking, hosting, and spending time in.

Frugal Foundations

- **Set up your kitchen for home cooking.** Investing in essential kitchen tools will make it easier and more fun for you and your family to do more cooking at home (see lists below). You don't need to invest in all of your kitchen tools and utensils at once. If there are items you need to make your kitchen optimal for cooking, keep an eye out for discounts and deals at garage sales, flea markets, and thrift stores.

- **Thick-bottomed stainless steel pots.** Quality pots are a bit of an investment, but they'll last forever if you take care of them. Stainless steel pots last so long that you can even pass them down to your children. My mom still uses the pots she was gifted as hand-me-downs from her grandmother—talk about frugal! These four pots will cover most of your cooking needs:
    - 1 large stock/soup pot
    - 1 large pasta pot
    - 1 medium saucepan
    - 1 small saucepan

- **Cast iron pans.** Just like stainless steel pots, cast iron pans can last a lifetime. Cast iron is noted for its even cooking and the delicious sear it gives to meat. Cast iron pans are oven-safe and versatile enough to cook anything from fried chicken and steak to pan breads and pizza. Lodge, Staub, and Le Creuset are high-quality brands. Look for second-hand cast iron at garage sales, thrift stores, and swap meets. It can take a bit of cleaning and oiling to bring them back to life—check out YouTube for videos on restoring and seasoning your cast iron. Cast iron pans to add to your collection include:

- o   12-in. deep-sided pan with sturdy handles on both sides
- o   Standard 8-in. pan
- o   10-in. square grill pan
- o   Shallow-sided pancake pan

- **Non-stick pans.** As great as cast iron is, it can't do everything—try making over-easy eggs in one of them! Non-stick pans are a great addition to your frugal kitchen because they make for easy clean-up and allow you to use less oil for dishes like sautés and stir-fries.
  - o   Sauté pan (12-in., 8-in., 6-in.)
  - o   Deep-sided brazier (10-in. to 12-in.)
  - o   Shallow-sided brazier (12-in. to 14-in.)

- **Sheet pans.** Also known as cookie sheets or baking trays, sheet pans are all-purpose metal (often non-stick) trays. These pans are great for baking, sheet-pan dinners, and batch-cooking ingredients like bacon. Thrift stores often have a wide selection of sheet pans in different sizes. They may look dingy and grubby, but you can bring any stainless steel sheet pan back to life with a Brillo pad, a mix of baking soda and vinegar, and a little elbow grease. The most useful sizes include:
  - o   Full-size (18×26 in.)
  - o   1/2-size (13×18 in.)
  - o   1/4-size (9 1/2×13 in.)

- **Casserole dishes.** Who doesn't love a good casserole? Warm, comforting, and delicious—and famously frugal-friendly. Thrift stores are (by far) the most frugal option for casserole dishes and other crockery. Popular brands for casserole dishes include Pyrex, Anchor, and Cuisinart. Start your casserole dish collection with the following sizes:
    - Family size (14×7 in.)
    - Regular weeknight size (9×11 in.)
    - Small-batch size (8×8 in.)
- **Useful utensils.** Most people don't want to be digging through drawers of gadgets like avocado scoops and garlic peelers while looking for basic tools like wooden spoons or whisks. Your kitchen "clean sweep" should have helped you reduce the number of useless utensils you have. As you build out your collection of practical utensils, aim for silicone or wood— especially if you have non-stick pans. Stainless steel utensils are well-suited for stainless steel or cast iron cookware. The following list is a good starting point to ensure your kitchen has the right utensils for most cooking tasks:
    - Full set of basic cutlery (large fork, small fork, tablespoon, teaspoon, butter knife, steak knife for each family member plus guests)
    - Silicone-tipped metal tongs (short- and long-handled)
    - Small and large whisks
    - Variety of wooden spoons
    - Silicone spatulas, flippers, large spoons, slotted spoons
    - Stainless steel spatulas, flippers, large spoons, slotted spoons
    - Silicone basting brush
    - Stainless steel potato masher
    - Kitchen shears

- o Pastry scraper
- o Wooden rolling pin
- o Measuring cups and spoons
- o Vegetable peeler
- o Carving fork
- o Stainless steel offset spatula
- o Serving spoons and forks (small and large)
- **Useful gadgets.** Although I lightly mock the frivolity of kitchen tools like banana slicers, some gadgets are really helpful to have in the kitchen. Not all of these tools are essential, but as you grow your home cooking repertoire, you may find it useful to add them to your collection:
  - o Can opener
  - o Stainless steel box grater
  - o Stainless steel or bamboo steamer
  - o Colander in several sizes
  - o Fine-mesh strainer in several sizes
  - o Citrus juicer
  - o Citrus zester
  - o Melon baller
  - o Ice cream scoops in several sizes (great for making meatballs and cookies)
  - o Garlic press
  - o Digital kitchen food scale
- **Mixing bowls.** It's important to have a selection of mixing bowls made from a few different materials. Different recipes need different types of bowls, so I recommend having a selection of each type in a variety of sizes:
  - o Stainless steel mixing bowls
  - o Hard plastic mixing bowls
  - o Glass mixing bowls (Pyrex, Anchor)

- **Quality, sharp knives.** Home cooking is more fun, easier, and safer when you work with quality knives that are kept sharp and properly honed. Quality kitchen knives don't have to be expensive. Victorinox is a very affordable brand and is the restaurant standard because they keep a good edge and are relatively light. To frugally build out your knife collection, check out thrift stores, garage sales, and flea markets for second-hand knife blocks and knife sets. Keep in mind that your knife set doesn't have to be matching. I've accumulated a mismatched set of Henckel and Wüsthof Trident knives over the years from sifting through the utensil bins at Goodwill each time I visit. I also recommend that you invest in a 2-sided wet sharpening stone. Check out YouTube for how to sharpen your own knives—it's simple and will save you money on having your knives sharpened in a shop. Aim to have the following kitchen knives in your collection:
  - o 12-in. chef's knife
  - o 10-in. utility knife (sometimes called a santoku knife)
  - o 8-in. utility knife
  - o Paring knife
  - o Serrated knife (sometimes called a bread knife)
  - o Honing steel
- **Transition to reusable kitchen linens.** Over the last few years, one of the most significant frugal habits we adopted was moving away from disposable paper towels and napkins for most of our daily cleaning needs. Although we were already using cotton kitchen towels (tea towels) for various purposes, we were still using paper towels frequently—as napkins with each meal or snack, for small spills, to sanitize the counters after meal prep, and to dry our hands after washing them. Our reusable kitchen linens were inexpensive to buy brand new (check out Amazon),

and we wash a big load of them every two weeks—so there isn't much soap, bleach, power, or water used to clean them. On sunny days, kitchen linens can also be easily hung on an outside wash line to dry. Look for white towels so they can be bleached. The following kitchen linens will help you reduce waste and the cost of disposable paper towels and napkins:

o **Tea towels.** We use tea towels for everything from wiping down the counter to laying over a rising bowl of bread dough. In our linen cupboard, we have about 40 of them.

o **Hand towels.** These are most often "half-towels" with a loop and button to hang them on a cupboard handle or oven door. Now, instead of reaching for paper towels to dry our clean hands, we reuse the cotton hand towels and replace them with fresh towels as needed.

o **Cloth napkins.** When you consider the paper napkin use of an average family of four eating three meals plus snacks every day, you could easily go through a few rolls of paper towel each week. Cloth napkins are inexpensive to buy (or, if you're crafty with a sewing machine, you can make them yourself)—and feel much better against your lips and skin than rough paper.

o **Dishcloths instead of sponges.** Let's face it: kitchen sponges are gross. They're used to clean up any manner of food—from raw eggs to meat juice—and the likelihood of the sponge being fully sanitized between uses is pretty low. Scrubber sponges can be useful for pots, pans, and stuck-on dishes, but for regular dishwashing, try reusable dishcloths instead. If you're a fan of knitting or crocheting, there are hundreds of patterns on Pinterest for reusable dishcloths.

Pantry Staples

Pantry staples are food items that are essential to have on hand at any given time—they make it easy to bring meals and recipes together without running to the grocery store every day. Pantry staples are the heroes of the kitchen because they can be used to whip up quick meals and help frugarians avoid the convenience pitfalls of ordering takeout or eating out at a restaurant. These items are most often used in scratch-cooking recipes and are also shelf-stable for long periods of time. Convenience foods in the frugal pantry are more often elements of a meal that make it easier to cook (mostly) from scratch—like jarred pasta sauce, cream soups, and canned meats. I'm not suggesting that you forgo all convenience foods (especially if you're a parent with small children), but rather stock your pantry with more of the base ingredients you would need to cook a similar item from scratch, so you have what you need when you have the time and motivation.

Frugal Foundations

- **Dry goods.** Dry goods are pantry items with a long shelf life (sometimes lumped in with the term "shelf stable").
  - Bottled water
  - Coffee, tea, and herbal tea
  - Boxed stuffing and breadcrumbs
  - Cake, pancake, biscuit, and muffin mixes
  - Boxed cereals
  - Cereal grains (oats, grits, cream of wheat, oat bran, etc.)
  - Crackers and cookies
  - Dried beans
  - Grains and rice (barley, quinoa, spelt, farrow, all varieties of rice, etc.)
  - Ramen noodles

o Pasta (spaghetti, linguini, fusilli, rigatoni, penne, lasagna, fettuccine, macaroni, etc.)

o Hot and cold powdered drink mixes (iced tea, lemonade, fruit punch, hot cider, hot chocolate, etc.)

o Flours (bread, pastry, all-purpose, whole wheat, semolina, etc.)

o Sugars (white, brown, golden, powdered, etc.)

o Leaveners (baking powder, baking soda, dry active yeast, cream of tartar, etc.)

o Syrups and honey (maple, agave, honey, molasses, corn syrup, etc.)

o Powdered milk and eggs

o Dried fruit (raisins, cranberries, apricots, apples, bananas, etc.)

o Dried vegetables (bell peppers, onions, carrots, celery, tomatoes, mushrooms, etc.)

- **Canned goods.** Canned goods have a long shelf life and are ideal to stock in case of emergencies. Make sure you also store an extra can opener.

  o Soups and stews (beef and barley, chicken and rice, mushroom, bean and bacon, beef stew, vegetable, tomato, etc.)

  o Beans (kidney, black, cannellini, navy, green, baked, chili, etc.)

  o Canned meat (corned beef, SPAM, potted ham, Vienna sausages, cooked ham, etc.)

  o Canned seafood (tuna, salmon, smoked oysters, sardines, kippers, etc.)

  o Milk (condensed milk, evaporated milk, infant formula, shelf-stable UHT milk, coconut milk, almond milk, etc.)

- o Canned vegetables (green beans, peas, corn, potatoes, carrots, beets, etc.)
- o Canned pickles (dill pickles, olives, artichokes, asparagus, sauerkraut, kimchi, etc.)
- o Canned tomatoes (whole, stewed, strained, pureed, diced, roasted, paste, sauce, etc.)

- **Condiments and sauces.** Condiments and prepared sauces are a great way for frugarians to jazz up the more basic (and sometimes plain) pantry staples. During hard times in the past, I've had to live off very basic food like rice and potatoes—but it was manageable with a little bit of soy sauce and ketchup. Check out wholesale retailers and discount grocers for great deals on these items.
  - o Ketchup
  - o Mustard (picnic, Dijon, grainy, honey mustard, English, etc.)
  - o Mayonnaise (regular, garlic, chipotle, pesto, etc.)
  - o Steak and BBQ sauces
  - o Salad dressings (ranch, Italian, balsamic, Greek, Thousand Islands, Caesar, etc.)
  - o Asian sauces (soy sauce, fish sauce, black bean, hoisin, teriyaki, sweet chili, Szechuan, peanut, sriracha, etc.)
  - o South Asian sauces (tandoori, butter chicken, coconut curry, vindaloo, etc.)
  - o Pasta sauces (marinara, Bolognese, alfredo, pesto, roasted red pepper, sun-dried tomato, etc.)
  - o Dessert sauces (hot fudge, caramel, strawberry, etc.)
  - o Flavourings and extracts (vanilla, almond, coconut, lemon, peppermint, etc.)
- **Baking supplies.** Having these items on hand makes it easy to prepare baked goods at home.

o   Muffin liners
o   Parchment paper
o   Aluminum foil
o   Brown cooking paper
o   Butcher's twine
o   Cheesecloth
o   Cooking spray

- **Herbs and spices.** An effective and inexpensive way for frugarians to add flavour to humble ingredients is with an assortment of herbs and spices. Even a modest collection can turn a simple $1 jar of generic pasta sauce into something flavorful and more homemade. A bit of turmeric and cumin added to a basic pot of rice turns it a vibrant yellow with an aroma well-suited for South Asian dishes. If you're just starting out with home cooking, look for inexpensive dried herbs and spices at the dollar store or local retail marts. Ethnic grocery stores also carry a wide selection of herbs and spices at very affordable prices.

  o   Herbs (parsley, sage, thyme, rosemary, cilantro, basil, oregano, chives, marjoram, savory, tarragon, etc.)
  o   Spices (black pepper, cinnamon, garlic powder, onion powder, Montreal steak spice, turmeric, ginger, cumin, chili powder, cloves, paprika, red pepper flakes, lemongrass, etc.)
  o   Salt (table, sea, flaked, Himalayan, kosher, pickling, etc.)

- **Cooking oils and vinegars.** Every frugal home cook should have an arsenal of cooking oils and acids in their pantry to allow them to create dressings, sauces, and marinades. Most recipes also include some form of oil or fat for cooking.

  o   Oils (olive, avocado, coconut, vegetable, sesame, etc.)
  o   Vinegars (distilled white, red wine, apple cider, malt, balsamic, rice wine, etc.)

Buying in Bulk

There's a reason why Costco has been so popular over the last 15 years. People are enamoured by the idea of buying items in massive quantities for less overall cost than if they were purchased individually. While I'm a fan of big box stores and club grocers for some items, these stores are not always the best place to buy bulk goods, since the larger volume doesn't always yield the most savings. By familiarizing yourself with the price per kilogram (or pound) found on the store shelf price tags and item price stickers, you'll be able to identify which size product will have the least expensive cost per gram (or ounce).

When you discover the least expensive option for a particular food or household item, you can purchase it in a large quantity knowing that, on a price-per-gram level, you're getting the best value. A good example of this is peanut butter. You may go to Costco and buy the 2 kg jumbo jar, thinking it's an amazing deal at $12.99—until you spot a 500 g jar for $2.49 at your local Aldi. Not only that, but from a usability perspective, it's much easier for little hands to grasp smaller jars and easier to rotate through your stockpile.

Frugal Foundations

- **Explore group purchases.** Group purchases can be an excellent way to buy items that you may not be able to afford on your own—they allow you to buy a large quantity at a discount because you can access bulk pricing. One of the most common group purchases is to buy a whole animal, have it butchered, with the cuts packed in vacuum-sealed poly bags. The freezer packs can then be divided among the group members. The price per pound/kilo will be much less than if those individual packs were purchased at retail prices from a grocery store. If you buy a whole pig, for example, you're going to end up with a few dozen individual packs of meat. By going in with a family member or some friends on the purchase price, you don't have to shell out $600 for a whole pig—you could contribute $150 and get a substantial amount of meat for that price point. This method also works well for any large-scale purchases that can be easily divided.

- **Buy pantry staples in bulk.** Shopping for pantry staples in bulk is an excellent way to reduce your food budget. Having a surplus of bulk items in your stockpile allows you to inexpensively keep a substantial amount of food on hand in case of a job loss, emergency, or other unforeseen circumstances. Traditional grocery stores typically offer most pantry items in a variety of sizes. If you check out the prices and see the per-pound/kilo breakdown, it's usually more expensive to buy the smaller packages. You can save even more money on items like rice, nuts, flour, oatmeal, pasta, and spices by shopping in your grocery store's bulk-bin section. In Canada, we have an entire store dedicated to bulk-bin shopping called Bulk Barn. If you have a similar retailer in your area, take advantage of it! If you're new to stocking pantry staples, it's also a great place to start because you can save money on a variety of essentials without having to buy huge quantities.

- **Buy direct from farmers.** When it comes to produce and meat, your best bet is to buy directly from farmers. Livestock farmers typically have great deals on whole, half, quarter, and multi-cuts of meat (beef, pork, lamb, bison, elk, venison, moose, etc.). Look for farmers who vacuum seal their meat—cuts wrapped in nothing but waxed brown paper can quickly become freezer-burnt. You may pay a bit extra for the shrink-wrap, but it will save you money in the long run—your meat will stay fresh, and you'll be able to buy a larger quantity since it will keep well in the freezer for years. This year, we purchased a whole pig from a farmer who raises grass-fed Berkshire pigs. The meat is so fresh and delicious! Buying our meat directly from the farmer in bulk gives us exceptional quality for much less money than the grocery store.

- **Explore liquidation centres for non-food items.** Wholesale retailers and liquidation centres are a great option for buying non-food items in bulk. When manufacturers change packaging design or sizes, any surplus of the old products are sent to various retailers across North America. The items available at these stores vary from week to week—that's part of the fun! Explore your local wholesaler for deals on household and personal items (laundry detergent, toilet paper, diapers, feminine hygiene products, lightbulbs, batteries, trash bags, etc.). Occasionally, they also stock pantry items.

- **Don't buy more than you can use.** Be cautious about buying huge quantities of perishable items. It may seem like a great deal at the time, but you're not going to save any money if you throw out a portion of your purchase because it expired. I expand more on this topic in the "Waste Not, Want Not" section below— strive to make sure that you're using any food or household items before they expire and not throwing away much (if anything).

Generic Brands

We're told through advertisements and product placement that the only acceptable products for families to use are name brands like Campbell's, Pepsi, Uncle Ben's, and Lipton. But the reality is that a lot of generic brands are actually produced in the same factories (on the same equipment and using the same ingredients) as their name-brand counterparts. For a fraction of the price, you can get equivalent (or sometimes better) quality food. By slowly integrating generic swaps into your family's grocery budget, you'll be making subtle changes that will have a lasting impact on your wallet.

Frugal Foundations

- **Be willing to try.** The first step of switching to generic brands is having the willingness to try. For too long, consumers have been told by the media that off-brands are somehow less than and reserved for lower-income shoppers who can't afford name-brand goods. Generic brands aren't designated for a certain income level—and their quality isn't necessarily lower because they're less expensive. As a new frugarian, it's time to brush aside any preconceived notions of what generic means. When I was on a limited budget in college, I changed my mindset and began viewing them as *frugal brands* instead of off-brands.

- **Swap one item at a time.** As you ease into your new frugal lifestyle, try out generic brands by starting slowly and swapping out a few of your favourite items for their generic equivalent. For example, if you make a family favourite casserole with Campbell's Cream of Mushroom Soup, try swapping out the soup for its generic counterpart and see if your family can tell the difference. Dollars to doughnuts—they won't even notice. Try this trick with a few items each shopping trip until you've swapped most of your food and pantry items for lower-cost generics. This frugal habit will also allow you to take advantage of sale-priced items, no matter the brand.

- **Keep a generic journal.** As you explore new generic options of your favourite foods, jot down which products you like the taste of—and which you don't. If you or your family don't like the taste of a certain brand, mark it down and try a different one. If there's an item or brand you really like, make note of that, too. That way, you can keep an eye out in flyers and clearance bins for when those brands go on sale. Depending on how much you like to make lists, you can even make a note of which store you found the item in and the price. You may notice that some of your favourite generic brands are consistently lower priced at certain stores.

- **Your little secret.** There's a funny scene in the TV series *Roseanne* where the children learn that Rosie has been using the same box of name-brand cornflakes for years—but filling it up with generic cereal so the kids wouldn't notice. You don't have to be that sneaky, but there's no need to announce to your family that you're making these subtle changes. If they balk at the taste of a generic item, you can make note of it in your journal and try another brand. If they don't notice, you can carry on cooking delicious frugal meals for your family with your new generic staples.

Pack it Up!

With all the home cooking you'll be doing as a new frugarian, you're going to have plenty of leftovers. To save money and time, make sure to pack up your leftover food for your kid's lunches or take it with you to work. This will not only help you avoid throwing out food that spoils before you can eat it, but it will also keep your lunches full of nourishing home-cooked fare. Packing hearty lunches is also a great way to prevent you from grabbing expensive takeout or going out to a restaurant. Any food or beverages that you bring with you when you're away from home also save you money. Hubby had a recent hospital stay, and I was shocked to pay $6 for a bottle of water from the vending machine. The next day, I brought a small cooler pack full of snacks and beverages from home to save on the cost of convenience. If you know you're going to be away from home during meal times, or long enough that you'll need a snack, plan ahead and pack it up!

Frugal Foundations

- **Pack school lunches.** Giving kids cash for cafeteria food every day can get expensive—and school meals aren't always the healthiest. Reusable insulated lunch bags and small storage containers are frugal ways to build the habit of bringing lunch from home. With a bit of planning, your children can enjoy meals they actually like, and you'll have peace of mind knowing the ingredients that went into each one. When packing lunches, focus on foods they're willing to eat that day. It's not frugal to find a full, untouched lunch after school because a picky eater wasn't interested. Check in with them each morning or let them pick from the week's leftovers. Remember that unopened packaged foods can go back into rotation, and many perishables can be used as snacks later in the day.

- **Pack work lunches.** Packing work lunches for you and your spouse is a great frugal option for your midday meal. Getting drawn into the office culture of eating out every day for lunch, or grabbing snacks and coffee several times each week, can easily set you up for overspending. Bringing meals, snacks, and beverages from home can help prevent you from hitting the nearby corner store for your afternoon sugar fix or the bagel counter for your breakfast. Even bringing a granola bar or piece of fruit from home can save you money on snacks—especially from cafeterias and vending machines that are usually very overpriced. Keep in mind that being frugal doesn't mean that you should never go out for lunch with colleagues or grab a quick snack on the run. It's about making it a habit to take your meals and snacks to work most days—while maintaining a social connection by going out a couple of times per month instead of multiple times each week.

- **Pack a cooler for outdoor events, road trips, and getaways.** Life is busy! But stopping for fast food or at a convenience store when we get hungry isn't just expensive—it's unhealthy. To save money on eating out, pack a lunch and snacks when you know you'll be away from home during mealtimes. By planning ahead and thinking about your agenda for the day, you can pack a frugal cooler with everything you need to stay fed and hydrated during your outing. Easy-to-pack snacks for the cooler include peanut butter and jelly sandwiches, cheese and crackers, fruit, muffins, granola bars, beef jerky, and pepperoni sticks. Depending on how long you'll be gone, tuna or egg salad bunwiches are always a hit! One of my favourite frugal tips is to keep a small stash of snacks in the centre console of our car. A simple protein bar or fruit leather can fill you up until you get home and have something more substantial to eat.

- **Invest in storage containers.** An assortment of storage containers will make it easy for you to pack up leftovers or divide meals and snacks into smaller, lunch-sized portions. Keep an eye out for containers at thrift stores and garage sales (especially for higher-end brands like Tupperware or Rubbermaid), or start collecting resealable plastic tubs from butter, sour cream, or yogurt. If you're buying your storage containers new, buy what you can afford. The dollar store is a good option for plastic containers that won't be reheated. For food you want to warm up, use glass containers with plastic lids.

- **Try "snack plate" lunches.** Some of my favourite lunches are those I throw together near the end of the month, when selection is limited before our next big grocery trip. I take the "mix and match" approach, with several small portions of the items that need to be eaten before they spoil. A few crackers with that last little bit of cheese. The last couple of pickles at the bottom of the jar. A mandarin orange from the back of the crisper, peeled and segmented. Thin slices of cold roast beef. A handful of cherry tomatoes. A tiny Snickers bar left over from Halloween. A selection of random items can come together into a quick and frugal lunchtime meal, full of variety and fun.

Meal Planning

If you've ever thought about a meal ahead of time and bought groceries based on what you needed for the recipes, you're already an old hand at meal planning. Meal planning as a frugarian is all about designing your meals for the week based on what you have in your pantry, fridge, and freezer—and what's on sale at your local grocery store. It's ideal for busy families, especially when there are extracurricular activities before or after dinner. By making an effort to align your meals with the least expensive ingredients you can find each week, you can keep your family nourished and satisfied while reducing your overall grocery budget.

Frugal Foundations

- **Plan meals based on sales.** If I could eat striploin steaks for dinner every night, I would. Like most families, however, that's not a realistic or affordable option. Instead of planning your meals based on the ingredients you prefer, try designing your meal plan around each week's sale-priced items. Discounted meat has the biggest money-saving potential. Look for deals on ground beef, less expensive cuts like chuck or blade steaks, or offcuts like bacon ends or deli scraps (great in sauces and casseroles). You can still work some of your favourite ingredients into your monthly rotation, but planning your meals around sales will help keep you on the frugal track.

- **Shop with a list.** How many times have you gone to the store without a list only to forget what you needed? How often have you wandered the aisles aimlessly, only to end up buying ingredients that you already had in your pantry or freezer? By making it a habit to write out exactly what you need when you go shopping, you'll be less tempted to make impulse purchases or buy expensive items that aren't in the budget for that week.

- **Start small and pre-plan one meal per week.** If you're a fan of online content, you've likely seen meal-planning and "large family batch cooking" videos on YouTube. In just 30 minutes of viewing time, you can watch frugal moms spend 15 hours on a Sunday making a whole month's worth of meals for their families (check out Amy Maryon—she's amazing). However, such ambition can be intimidating, overwhelming, and off-putting. To ease yourself into meal planning, start with one meal per week, like supper on a Tuesday. The following week, try planning two of your supper meals, and so on.

- **Meal plan with leftovers in mind.** One of the major frugal benefits of meal planning is leftovers. As you design your meal plan, be mindful to include recipes that will either yield leftovers of the dish (such as a giant casserole) or include an ingredient that can be used for multiple other meals (such as a large roasted chicken). If you roast a chicken on Sunday, you have the potential to use leftovers for several days. You can use the meat for sandwiches, add it to a pasta sauce, or make some quick quesadillas. The leftover chicken bones can be used to make a flavourful base for chicken noodle soup. Whatever you decide to cook, go into each session with the mindset of: cook once, eat twice—or thrice!

- **Get your kids involved.** On the nights that are particularly busy for you and your family, such as when your spouse works late, or the kids are involved with extracurricular activities, enlist the help of older children to help get meals on the table. This is not only a great way to begin teaching your children how to cook, but it also takes some of the burden off you. Even if they aren't yet comfortable using the stove, they can help out before you get home by laying out ingredients for the recipe and washing or preparing the vegetables for you to cook. An electric frying pan can be a great way to get your teenage children involved in the cooking process. Together, you can wash, chop, and prepare the ingredients for the meal the night before so your child can learn to cook simple dishes on their own—like homemade hamburger helper or beef stroganoff. Learning to cook basic dishes will also help your kids learn to love home cooking and save money on their food bill as they become young adults.

Batch Cooking

Anyone who has come home from a long day of work and thrown a couple of frozen pizzas into the oven for supper can appreciate the benefits of batch cooking. Batch cooking is simply making delicious home-cooked meals ahead of time and freezing them so they can be easily prepared and enjoyed later. Batch cooking can be as simple as making a double recipe of dinner to have leftovers for lunch a few times later in the week—or it could be something more elaborate, like baking and freezing a dozen loaves of bread for your family to eat throughout the month. Batch cooking not only saves time on those nights when you don't want to prepare a meal from scratch, but it also saves a lot of money that would typically be spent ordering delivery or dining out.

Frugal Foundations

- **Double-batch your meals.** My favourite benefit of batch cooking is reducing the pile of dirty dishes and cutting the amount of time spent in the kitchen. You're already cooking anyway, so why not spend the time to prepare a bit more—and have double the amount of cooked food afterward. Double-batching your recipes and saving the rest for another day is also a great way to start building your freezer meal stockpile.

- **Take advantage of sales and discounts.** To attract shoppers, grocery stores typically have certain items steeply discounted in their flyers each week—and many of those items are designed to be used together in recipes. A good example of this is curry chicken. It's common for the chicken breast, sauce, coconut milk, rice, and naan bread to be on sale at the same time. When we notice several items for the same recipe on sale, we stock up. Trust me—recipes made with discounted ingredients taste so much better than if you had bought the items at full price.

- **Invest in reusable baking pans and casserole dishes.** One of the recent trends in meal planning has been to batch cook using thin aluminum baking pans and casserole trays from the dollar store. The meals are stored, frozen, and reheated in the same tray—then tossed in the garbage after the meal. While the trays may be convenient, they're not frugal or eco-friendly. Sturdy, reusable baking pans, trays, and casserole dishes can be purchased from hardware stores and retail marts such as Canadian Tire or Target. Watch for them to go on sale or look in the clearance section for discounts. Keep an eye out at garage sales and thrift stores for even better deals—and don't be scared off by a bit of dirt and grime. Steel wool, Bar Keepers Friend, and a little elbow grease can revive even the most tired-looking pans.

- **Batch cook recipes that freeze well.** As you cook more meals from scratch and freeze your leftovers, you'll begin to notice which items tend to freeze and reheat well, such as soups, sauces, raw doughs, and casseroles—and which items don't, such as potatoes, pasta, and some vegetables. With each new batch cooking session, make note of the recipes you and your family enjoyed the most when they were reheated, as well as those meals that didn't quite hit the mark the second time around.

Meat Alternatives

One of the most frugal ways to hack your family's food budget is to switch from a predominantly meat-based diet to one that integrates a variety of meat alternatives. Foods such as beans, lentils, and pulses are ideal meat substitutes, while eggs are a nutritious and affordable option for animal-based protein. Saving money on meat also frees up funds for other grocery and pantry items. In our family, we typically eat a meat-based diet. However, over the last several years, we've made an effort to choose less expensive cuts and eat them a few times per week instead of daily. Our favourite meat alternative is definitely eggs, but we also frequently eat beans, peas, and tofu.

Frugal Foundations

- **Use meat as an accent—not the main attraction.** Meat is often seen as the centrepiece of a meal, and it's not uncommon to eat some form of meat multiple times per day. Although meat is very nutritious and an essential part of your daily macronutrient requirements, it is very expensive when compared to other food items in your grocery cart. When you adopt a frugal mindset, you'll start to see meat as more of a co-star in your meals instead of the main attraction. Consider a typical dinner for a family of four. Instead of having a large chicken breast for each person, choose a dish like stir-fry or chicken pot pie that uses one or two chicken breasts for the whole meal.

- **Beans, the magical fruit.** The more you eat, the more money you'll have in your wallet. Beans are truly magical in that they provide the essential building blocks of protein that your body needs to thrive. As a bonus, they're also a fraction of the cost of animal-based protein. The versatility and nutrition of beans make them a staple in many different parts of the world—so you'll be able to find bean recipes in any of the flavour profiles you enjoy. From chili and baked beans to hummus and curry, strive to make beans your primary meat alternative. When you're stocking your pantry, choose a variety of both canned and dried beans. Dried beans are much cheaper than canned and are considered non-perishable—ideal for stockpiling and emergency preparedness.

- **Learn to love lentils.** Lentils are a legume similar to beans in their nutrition, flavour profile, and versatility. In many countries, lentils are revered for their nutrient density and affordability. Whether you cook them down into a rich, warming soup or prepare them al dente to add to salads or other recipes, lentils are a frugal staple. Along with their indefinite shelf life, lentils have a comfort and heartiness to them that makes meals delicious and filling even on a tight budget.

- **Experiment with tofu.** Tofu has a reputation for being squishy and flavourless, but its range of textures and neutral flavour make it ideal for frugal cooking. Tofu is a pressed curd made from soybeans, and it's typically available in extra firm, firm, medium, soft, and silken varieties. Tofu is a perfect protein alternative—it's inexpensive, versatile, and increases the overall volume of dishes to make them more filling and satisfying. We like to sear chunks of firm tofu in a bit of rendered animal fat like tallow or lard and add a bottled (or homemade) Asian stir-fry sauce to coat. We then serve it with rice and steamed vegetables. Silken tofu is delicious in desserts or smoothies and gives a boost of protein for very few calories. Look for tofu in the produce section of the grocery store.

- **Make eggs a main source of protein.** Eggs have been called nature's "perfect food", and for good reason. They're nutrient dense, full of healthy omega-3 fats, and are easy to prepare. Eggs are incredibly versatile with countless preparation options—from fried and hard-boiled to shakshuka and huevos rancheros. They can be added to Asian noodle dishes or scrambled into fried rice. They can even be cooked thin like a crepe and sliced into noodles! However you decide to cook them, always strive to buy the best eggs you can afford. In Canada, we pay around $7 (CAD) per dozen (2025) for organic, free-range eggs. We spend more for higher-quality eggs since they're such an important staple protein for us. The way we look at it, if we were buying the equivalent protein in beef, pork, or chicken, we would be paying substantially more—so for us, it's worth it. When Hubby and I were starting out as a couple, we bought generic factory eggs as inexpensively as possible and enjoyed them. But as we started to make more meals with eggs as the centrepiece, such as breakfast for dinner, we started to buy better eggs. To save money on high-quality eggs, you can also buy them directly from farmers or at farmers' markets. To go the extra frugal mile, you can even raise backyard chickens if your city or town bylaws allow them.

Love Your Leftovers

I was at work the first time I heard of someone who didn't like leftovers. A few of us were reheating our lunches that were left over from the previous night's dinners, and one of our coworkers said, "I can't believe you eat leftovers". I confusedly asked, "Wait a minute. You don't eat leftovers?" to which she replied, "No way! I hate reheated food".

While still wearing my disbelief on my face, I asked if she just makes sure to cook the exact amount her family needs for dinner each night. My stomach dropped, and I was genuinely shocked when she admitted that she threw the leftover food in the garbage. It's one of those things I never gave a lot of thought to before that conversation. I just assumed that everyone packs up their leftover food whenever they make a meal. But not everyone saves their leftovers—they are literally throwing their money away.

In our family, we pack up all of our leftover food regardless of how much remains. It could be a quarter of a leftover potato chopped up and used in a frittata, or a little piece of steak that makes its way into a spicy cheese quesadilla. No matter the food, there's always a way to use it up. I understand that reheating food in the microwave isn't always the most palatable option—that's why we typically heat leftovers in the oven or air fryer. If you haven't tried an air fryer yet, I highly recommend it. It's a timesaver and gives you oven-quality meals in a fraction of the time it would take in a traditional oven. It also saves on energy costs and reduces the amount of expensive oils needed to achieve a golden-brown colour and delicious flavour.

One of the primary ways we maximize our food budget is to cook extra on purpose to have leftovers for future meals. We often pack leftovers for lunches, but we also save some of the food to make it easier on ourselves on weeknights. A favourite "leftover" is beef and pork meatballs because we can make a large batch in the oven on Sunday and use those balls for several meals throughout the week, like spaghetti and meatballs, Swedish meatballs, or as a base for Greek pita wraps (also known as gyros).

Frugal Foundations

- **Learn to love leftovers.** There's no shame in eating leftovers or taking leftovers from the night before to work for lunch. As you transition to home cooking most of your meals, you'll naturally accumulate leftovers. If you don't enjoy food reheated in the microwave, try warming it in the oven or on the stovetop. We preheat our oven to 350°F, dish out the portions of leftovers into a baking dish, add a bit of water, and cover tightly with foil. Some leftovers even taste better the second time around. Lasagna, soups, stews, and chili are all tastier the next day after the flavours have had a chance to meld.

- **Get creative.** As you become more experienced with home cooking, your ingenuity will grow, and you'll learn to create new meals with leftover ingredients. Hubby and I love experimenting with our leftovers—to the point that we challenge each other to see who can make the tastier dish. There's a special kind of pride that comes with a comment like, "Oh, this is so delicious! What's in this?" when it's made up of ingredients leftover from the last few suppers.

- **Embrace the frugal frittata.** Just like *The Lion King* song, *Hakuna Matata*, a frugal frittata means "no worries". Frittatas are an excellent way to use up leftovers. Simply go through your fridge at the end of the week and gather up all of your bits and pieces—ingredients like chunks of onion and peppers, leftover bacon, those last couple of mushrooms that you need to use before they go bad, a hunk of cooked potato, a small cube of cheddar cheese, and the tops of green onions that are starting to wilt. Pretty much any leftover food or scrap vegetables can be used in a frittata. I've made delicious frittatas out of leftover spaghetti and meatballs, leftover pork fajitas, and even leftover charcuterie from a holiday platter. A frugal frittata—no worries!

Waste Not, Want Not

It's not surprising that wasting anything—especially food—is completely contrary to the ideals of the frugal lifestyle. One of your goals as a frugarian should be to get as much use out of an item as possible before it no longer has value or purpose. In terms of food, you should strive to get as much value for your food dollar as possible. The easiest way to stretch your food budget is to make sure that you don't throw out prepared food or allow fresh food to go bad before you use it. When you consider how much food an average family wastes, it's really quite shocking.

"In 2017, the National Zero Waste Council conducted research on household food waste in Canada, and the results were astonishing:

- 63% of the food Canadians throw away could have been eaten
- For the average Canadian household, that amounts to 140 kilograms (~308 pounds) of wasted food per year—at a cost of more than $1,100 per year" (14).

For anyone's monthly food budget, 63% is a considerable amount of money to be throwing in the trash. But food wastage can occur for a variety of reasons, from buying more food than you need for the week to being unable or unprepared to consistently transform those ingredients into meals. Another common problem is being busy or tired. At the end of a long day, we know it's easier to hop on a delivery app and order food than to prepare a meal from scratch and clean up afterwards. Oftentimes, even with the best meal-planning intentions, we take the route of least resistance—and the food we bought for the week ends up being forgotten, pushed aside, and left to spoil at the back of the fridge. Using up as much of your groceries as you can before they get thrown away should be one of your primary food goals as a frugarian.

Frugal Foundations

- **Meal plan.** One of the easiest ways to prevent food waste is to meal plan. This helps ensure that you're using up food from your pantry and freezer and only buying the ingredients you need to prepare that week's meal plan recipes. In our household, we strive to know what's in the fridge, what needs to be used up, and what is close to expiring. We're not perfect (sorry, moldy cucumbers at the back of the crisper), but whenever we throw food away, we consider how we could have planned our meals so all of the older food was used up first. Certain convenience meal plans, like Crock-Pot dinners or sheet pan meals, can be found on YouTube. A favourite frugal creator of ours is *That Lisa Dawn*.

- **Use up older food before you buy new.** As you push your shopping cart around the grocery store, it's common to be tempted by "new" everywhere you look—bright, colourful, fresh, and enticing. Without a plan, it can be easy to forget that you either don't need the ingredients for that week's recipes or that you already have those items at home in your stockpile. By using frugal techniques like making a list, meal planning, and shopping your pantry, you'll be limiting food wastage by replacing only the items you need. Rotating food in your pantry, fridge, and freezer will ensure that older food is always used first and will also free up room for new groceries with a longer shelf life.

- **Get creative with "kitchen sink" soup.** Before our big monthly shopping trip, we often make "kitchen sink" soup—a mixed vegetable (and sometimes meat) soup using all of the older ingredients in the fridge and pantry that are close to expiring. We scrounge through every nook and cranny of the fridge and freezer for ingredients like leftover bacon fat, limp carrots and celery, leftover sausage, or cooked pasta from the night before. We rummage through the pantry for older foods, like onions that may be soft and need several layers of skin removed, cans of old beans or diced tomatoes, or shriveled potatoes with a few sprouting eyes. We clean and chop the ingredients into bite-sized pieces and toss them all into a big soup pot with some homemade stock and herbs and seasonings to taste. Some of the best soups we've made have been "kitchen sink" soups. Doing a clear-out like this also frees up your fridge and pantry for new, fresh groceries.

- **Freeze vegetable scraps and bones for stock.** If you prepare a recipe that yields a lot of vegetable scraps, you can freeze them to make soup or stock later. We keep a large zip-top freezer bag in our freezer at all times and add scraps to it whenever we cook. To get the best stock possible, we only add classic stock ingredients like onions, carrots, celery, and tomatoes, as well as herbs like parsley. We never add items like broccoli, cabbage, cauliflower, or asparagus because they have such strong flavours. If you want to be extra frugal, you can keep a separate bag for those vegetables and use them to make a pungent stock for recipes like broccoli cheddar sauce or cauliflower soup. The freezer is also a great place to store leftover bones. If we cook a whole roast chicken or a ham, we always save the bones in a freezer bag. We also keep bones from smaller cuts like pork chops or T-bone steaks. When we plan to make homemade soup, we grab a few bags of frozen veggie scraps and add them to the saved bones to create a fresh and delicious stock for pennies.

- **Save rendered fats.** If you've ever fried a pack of bacon, you're aware of the incredible amount of fat left in the pan after cooking. Some people soak up the fat with a paper towel, while others keep a glass jar under the sink and throw it away once it's full of grease. For frugarians, rendered fats are liquid gold. Other than fresh meat, oils and fats for cooking are among the most expensive food items you purchase. However, many of the meats you cook day-to-day render fats that can be used in other recipes. When you cook meats such as bacon, ground beef, pork chops, sausages, and skin-on chicken, pour the leftover fat into a glass container and store it in the fridge. There is nothing like hashbrowns cooked in sausage fat or onions caramelized in chicken fat. Some recipes, like baking powder biscuits or pie crusts, actually call for lard as an ingredient. In the post-war era, my dad used to spread bacon grease on bread instead of butter (it's delicious) because it was a free by-product of their weekly bacon fry-up. Stored properly in the fridge, clean fat rendered from pork cuts (lard), beef cuts (tallow), or chicken (schmaltz) will last for many months, as will bacon fat. Fat from ground meats or sausage will last up to two weeks, so use it quickly.

- **Save condiment packs.** While I recommend cooking from scratch whenever possible, the reality is most of us still occasionally eat out or order takeout. That doesn't mean you can't still be frugal! When you place your order, ask for extra condiments if they're free of charge with your purchase (be cautious, because some restaurants now charge for them).

Common condiments include sugar, creamers, salt, pepper, mayonnaise, ketchup, hot sauce, vinegar, mustard, and BBQ sauce. As frugarians, we want to get the best deals and save money, but we also want to be honest. I would never recommend that you take condiments without making a purchase, or suggest that you load up your tray with packets just because they're "free with purchase". For example, if you ask for extra ketchup and they give you five packets—that's much different than helping yourself to fifteen. Being mindful and honest with how you collect condiments allows you to save money without crossing the line—it's a small, thoughtful habit that adds up over time. Another frugal tip for condiments is to let family members know that you save them. Many households naturally collect condiment packets and are more than happy to share with others.

- **Use up condiment packets first in recipes.** We have a small drawer in our cupboard for condiment packets and dipping sauces. Whenever I'm making a recipe that has one of those ingredients, I always draw from the condiment drawer first. Whether it's a bunch of ketchup packets mixed into a meatloaf, leftover packs of soy sauce added to a marinade, or honey mustard spread as a glaze on baked chicken, consider those packets as part of your pantry—and use them up before you open a new big bottle. You'll find those little packets are also a great addition to packed lunches (especially hot sauce and ketchup).

Expiration and Best Before Dates

When you buy packaged perishable goods from a grocery store, the items typically have a date stamp on them—which either signifies the "best before" date or an expiration date. As a frugarian, it's essential to understand the distinction. While the goods may still be edible, the best before date refers to when peak freshness starts to decline and impacts the taste and quality of the product. The expiration date, meanwhile, is when a product is no longer suitable or safe to consume. Packaged crackers or chips are examples of foods that taste best when eaten before their best before date. Expiration dates, on the other hand, are often found on dairy products, fermented foods, and various meats and meat products.

A major benefit of best before dates for frugarians is the availability of products in the clearance section or as markdown items. Since the items aren't expired, you can use them to supplement your meal plan and lower your grocery bill for the month.

Frugal Foundations

- **Learn to distinguish between date stamps.** The best before date signifies the date by which the food should be eaten for optimal taste and freshness. On packaging, the date is typically prefaced with "BB" (e.g., BB2025/01/31). The expiry date signifies the date after which the food is no longer safe to consume and should be discarded. This date is usually shown with "EXP" before the date (e.g., EXP2025/01/31).

- **Avoid consuming items past their expiration date.** As you check out the clearance bins, or even your own pantry shelves, be cautious of expiration dates. If you notice expired goods at home, discard them since those dates represent when the food is no longer safe to consume. If you come across expired items in a store, be sure to avoid them—and notify a clerk that they are no longer saleable.

- **Use caution with clearance meat.** Most grocery stores have a clearance section in their meat departments. As a frugarian, discounted meat is a great way to add protein to your meals for a fraction of the cost of fresh meat that was just put out. However, take caution when purchasing discounted meat past its best before date—and definitely avoid it if it's expired. There are too many anecdotal stories of people who ended up with food poisoning, sometimes getting extremely ill, from expired meat bought on sale. Risking your health isn't worth a bit of extra savings.

- **Use the sniff test.** Regardless of the dates printed on cans, stamped on the side of the box, or printed on the label, it's always a good practice to smell your perishable items before consuming them. A quick sniff can let you know right away if the food is "off"—inedible foods often smell sour, pungent, or just plain foul. If it doesn't smell fresh or like something you would eat, toss it. When in doubt, throw it out!

Food Banks

During lean times or when an emergency causes financial strain, it can be difficult for some families to meet their needs for food and nourishment. Designed to help members of the community who are in temporary need, food banks are typically funded through municipal grants or programs offered through various religious organizations. According to Food Banks Canada, "in March 2023, there were almost 2 million visits to food banks across Canada, representing a 32% increase compared to March 2022, and a 78.5% increase compared to March 2019, which is the highest year-over-year increase in usage ever reported" (15).

Food banks are invaluable resources for those times when you need extra support with groceries and basic personal hygiene items. As an essential service, food banks should only be used when you and your family are truly in need. Abuse of the system is common, and it's essential that you do not use food banks as a way to save money on food, but instead as a means for you and your family to survive during difficult times.

Frugal Foundations

- **Don't be afraid to ask for help.** The food bank exists for a reason, and there is no shame in seeking their services when you need a helping hand. I've had to rely on the food bank several times in my life and never once felt ashamed about it. In fact, I was so inspired by their generosity and support during those times of personal struggle that I now contribute to my local food pantry to help others facing similar challenges.

- **Focus on simple and hearty meals.** Food bank hampers are often packed to make it easy for you to combine ingredients into nourishing and filling meals. For example, if your box has noodles, tuna, canned peas, and cream of mushroom soup, you can make something like a lazy tuna casserole. A can of chunky beef stew served over a bed of plain white rice makes for a delicious and filling meal that also reheats well. A can of chickpeas, a jar of pasta sauce, and a package of pasta combine to make a delicious and filling meal packed with protein. *The Quaint Housewife* (16) on YouTube is an excellent resource for food bank hamper meal ideas.

- **Supplement with low-cost staples.** If you can afford to spend a small amount of money on groceries, focus on staple foods that are inexpensive and calorie-dense. Rice, oatmeal, pasta, dried beans, lentils, and instant potatoes are base ingredients that will help you stretch the contents of your food hamper over multiple meals—and keep you feeling full longer.

- **Get creative with food hamper items.** With the influx of families and individuals using food banks, supplies at some locations can be quite limited. This demand may result in you receiving a hamper with seemingly mismatched ingredients. Thinking outside of the box can help keep your meals interesting and prevent boredom when you're temporarily eating meals without much variety. A spoonful of raspberry jam mixed into your morning oatmeal is a delicious option when sugar is in short supply. A small jar of salsa mixed with plain rice and canned tuna makes a bright and fresh filling for burritos or tacos. A drained can of corn combined with cream of chicken soup makes a tasty and comforting sauce for cooked pasta.

- **Show gratitude and give back.** Once you're in a financial position to donate to charity, consider supporting a local food bank or hamper program in your area. We give to the Edmonton Food Bank because they helped me through a difficult time as a young adult. It's not much, but I'm grateful to be able to support others in my community. Instead of a financial contribution, you can donate your time by helping to organize incoming donations or packing groceries into hampers for others to pick up.

Gardening

There's something so satisfying about plucking a cherry tomato off the vine and popping it into your mouth, knowing that you grew it yourself from a tiny seed. The process of sprouting, nurturing, and watering plants—from their first bit of green poking through the soil to their last harvest—directly rewards the amount of effort put in. The skill and art of gardening is seeing a resurgence as people gravitate toward a more sustainable and frugal way of life. Many of us remember fondly the gardens of our parents and grandparents, small patches of the backyard dedicated to fresh produce like strawberries, lettuce, and green onions. As a child, I had no idea those plots of earth were remnants of so-called Victory Gardens, planted to sustain families through the food rationing and financial hardship of wartime. The gardens fed both people and small animals, with many families raising backyard chickens and rabbits. Vegetable scraps were also used as compost to fertilize the next year's crop.

Beware of the common misconception that you need a massive backyard to have a successful garden. The reality is that anyone can have a garden in any amount of space. If you get creative with containers and position them to get a decent amount of sunlight, there are plenty of options for sustainable crops. I've grown herbs on my kitchen windowsill, and green onions and tomatoes on a balcony in small terracotta pots. I wasn't growing a huge amount of food, but I was building a small container garden centred around expensive herbs that would add a ton of fresh flavour to frugal homecooked meals—basil, mint, chives, thyme, rosemary, and oregano.

Hubby and I currently have a small backyard, but we're able to grow a substantial amount of food using raised beds and food-safe plastic containers. We use 20 litre (~5.3 gallon) buckets for potatoes, cucumbers, and tomatoes, and 5 litre (~1.3 gallon) buckets for lettuce, beans, green peppers, green onions, and herbs. We also spent several years observing sunlight patterns in the backyard to determine the optimal planting locations for high- and low-light plants. Over time, we also determined which produce grows well in our climate (cucumbers, peas, beans, and potatoes) and which plants struggle and aren't worth growing (turnips, red peppers, large tomatoes, and broccoli).

Frugal Foundations

- **Start small.** I was a big Martha Stewart fan in my youth. This created preconceived notions that you needed acres of land to garden on, and that you couldn't have a successful harvest without planting dozens of different crops. As an adult, I quickly learned that you can supplement your food supply with a small, modest garden. Simple-to-grow vegetables like lettuce, herbs, and green onions are excellent starter crops. As you plan your first small garden, consider how much various vegetables cost at the grocery store. From a frugal perspective, it may not make sense to take up a corner of your balcony with a container of potatoes when you can buy a 20-pound bag for $10. On the other hand, herbs are notoriously expensive to buy but simple to grow in a small footprint.

- **Keep it contained.** With the majority of the world's population living in urban centres, most of us don't have much space in our backyards—or have backyards at all. Container gardens are an ideal way to save space, maximize yield, reduce water usage, and minimize pesky invaders. If you're interested in container gardening, ensure your containers are food-grade (i.e., HDPE) and suitable for growing food. Check out ReUse centres and flea markets for containers and pots for planting.

- **Plant crops that grow well in your area.** You may live in Canada and long for fresh oranges, or in the southern U.S. and crave Saskatoon berries—but the reality is that not all garden crops grow well in every climate. By focusing on the types of fruits and vegetables that thrive in your local conditions, you'll improve your chances of a successful harvest while avoiding the cost of wasted seeds and time.

- **Plant crops that store well long term.** Although eating produce straight off the vine is one of the major perks of growing a garden, it's important to diversify plant types to ensure you have fresh produce long after summer is over. Without preservation, fresh vegetables like tomatoes, peppers, zucchini, and spinach are best eaten soon after harvesting. Winter crops, however, can be stored for several months in your basement's cold pantry or the refrigerator. Winter crops include various squash (spaghetti, acorn, pumpkin, and butternut), potatoes, parsnips, carrots, turnips, beets, onions, and garlic.

- **Learn to glean and dry your seeds.** At the end of each growing season, most plants flower and produce seeds. Buying organic seeds from a wholesaler like Westcoast Seeds can cost several dollars per packet—a price that adds up when you're planting a full garden. Learning how to glean seeds from different fruits and vegetables is a fun and frugal way to perpetuate your garden for free. Cucumbers, beans, peas, peppers, tomatoes, cilantro, dill, carrots, and parsnips are easy-to-glean vegetables, perfect for new gardeners. Check out *The Seedkeepers* on YouTube (17) for step-by-step tutorials.

- **Check out seeds from the library.** With a focus on food security, knowledge sharing, and sustainability, many libraries now offer "seed banks". The diverse collections of seeds enable community members to start their own small gardens for free. To keep stock levels up, public library seed banks often accept gleaned seeds from local members. In the past, we've shared seeds from our garden as a way to frugally contribute back to our community and inspire others to embrace gardening.

- **Buy supplies and tools second hand.** Gardening supplies can be expensive, and there's typically an upfront cost for the equipment needed in your first year. Fortunately, gardening supplies often turn up at garage sales, ReUse centres, thrift stores, and eco-stations for bargain prices. From shovels, rakes, hoes, and trellises to chicken wire, buckets, and flower pots, using second-hand supplies is a frugal way to reduce the cost of your garden project. As a bonus, many cities and towns offer free bags of compost for citizens to use in their home gardens.

Gleaning and Foraging

If you've ever wandered along a country road or urban parkway and discovered a big bush of ripe berries, you know the joy of hand-picking the fruit and savouring the freshness of each bite. Perhaps without realizing it, you were practicing the frugal art of gleaning and foraging—extracting resources and food from trees, plants, and fungi in your area. Many cities and towns have foraging groups where members explore their local parklands and public spaces for edible plants and mushrooms. As you gain knowledge and experience, gleaning and foraging can become a viable and sustainable way to supplement your food stores.

Hubby and I have gleaned raspberries and blackberries from brambles in the river valley and have also picked apples and cherries from trees in city parks. We're still in the early stages of learning plant identification, but one of our goals is to gain enough experience in this area to be able to teach others. Foraging groups are an ideal way to learn, but libraries also provide a wealth of information and resources. Many branches offer free courses on plant identification and books on topics such as gleaning strategies, what grows in your area, and when the produce is ripe and ready for picking.

Be cautious before you eat any foraged plants, fruit, or mushrooms, and ensure you are with an expert with knowledge of your area and experience consuming foraged edibles. This is particularly important when dealing with mushrooms. **Do not eat any mushrooms that have not been properly identified by an expert in mycology.**

Frugal Foundations

- **Find fellow foragers.** With the popularity of homesteading and self-sustainability on the rise, many frugal foragers have begun workshops and walking tours of their local natural parklands. Through hands-on experiences, they teach others how to identify plants and help ensure they avoid eating anything poisonous or from an area that is not permitted. Check your local social media for meetups in your area.

- **Seek out fruit and nut trees on public lands.** Depending on where you live, and your region's climate, any number of fruit- and nut-bearing trees may be nearby. Most cities feature a variety of community parks that contain trees with edible fruits such as apples, crab-apples, cherries, peaches, and plums. Others may contain edible nuts like walnuts, acorns, and hazelnuts. Trees in southern climates may bear more exotic fruit such as avocados, lemons, and oranges. Contact your local municipal council to see if the public is allowed to glean from those trees. Many municipalities encourage the public to pick the fruit and intentionally plant fruit-bearing trees for that purpose.

- **Forage for fallen fruit.** Fallen fruit is one of those hidden gems that rarely gets much attention, even in frugal circles. Maybe it stems from the stigma of the fruit being rotten or not fresh, since it's on the ground. But fallen fruit is often the most delicious since it tends to release from the branch at peak ripeness. It's an ideal frugal food resource in summer since you don't need a ladder or any picking equipment to harvest it. All you need is a basket, bucket, or sack to gather fruit found in your area's public gardens and natural parklands.

- **Keep track of special spots.** Different areas have just the right conditions for certain types of plants to thrive, like creek beds for wild watercress or wooded groves for choke-cherries. As you glean and forage in your region, note any locations where you've found plentiful produce. Maybe it's a giant blackberry bramble down by the river or a 50-year-old pear tree on the edge of town. Keeping track of those special spots year after year will provide noticeable savings on your summer grocery bill.

- **Leave some for others.** Making sure that you don't glean a tree bare is a common bit of foraging etiquette. Since there are others in your community who could also benefit from the bounty, take only what you feel is a reasonable amount—such as a few pints of blackberries or a small basket of apples.

Canning and Preservation

As you adapt to your new frugal lifestyle, you may naturally gravitate toward more sustainable home and lifestyle activities. When I consider what "sustainable living" means to me, the ability to preserve food is at the top of my list. Whether you cultivate a backyard garden or buy fresh produce directly from farmers, preserving your summer harvest allows you to enjoy the bounty well into spring. Some of the more complex food preservation methods, such as pressure canning, can be daunting, but there are plenty of beginner-friendly options to get you started. Your preservation planning should also be flexible because successful crops tend to vary from year to year. With an arsenal of traditional and modern techniques, you can transform bumper crops into shelf-stable foodstuffs for your pantry.

Frugal Foundations

- **Start with soups.** At the end of the growing season, nutritious vegetable soups are a frugal way to preserve your garden harvest for the colder months. We typically make a massive batch of minestrone and freeze it in 1-litre mason jars. To effectively "freezer can", fill your jars only two-thirds of the way full to allow them to expand when frozen. Frugal soups that freeze and reheat well include potato and leek, broccoli and cheddar, mixed vegetable, butternut squash, carrot and ginger, borscht, zucchini and pepper, and many others. Keep in mind that broth-based soups freeze much better than creamy varieties. YouTube is a great resource for recipes, and you can search for videos based on your most plentiful crop.

- **Have fun with flash-freezing.** Whenever we have a surplus of green beans, carrots, peas, or zucchini, we blanch them in boiling water for a couple of minutes and then dunk them in an ice-water bath to stop the cooking process. To prepare bags of frozen vegetables, similar to those sold at the grocery store, we individually freeze the blanched vegetables by laying them in a single layer on a parchment-lined sheet pan and placing them in the freezer. Once they're frozen, we bag the vegetables in large zip-top freezer bags. You can mix and match them, like peas with carrots, or pack a single vegetable variety in each bag.

- **Learn from others.** As you build up your frugal community, you'll likely get to know people who are experienced with canning. Whether they learned from their elder family members, friends, or took a canning class, fellow frugarians are often eager to share the methods of this lost art with others. Don't be afraid to reach out and ask for advice or even to help out with one of their canning sessions. You can also check out your local library for beginner canning information sessions to learn the process step-by-step in a community kitchen.

- **Start with water bath canning.** If you're new to canning, start small with simple water bath canning. All you need is a pot large enough to submerge the jars in at least six inches of water, sanitized glass mason jars, brand-new lids, and jar rings. Most of the items needed for canning can be purchased second-hand at thrift stores or garage sales—especially the large canning pots, which I often see at Goodwill. Mason jars are also a good find at flea markets and estate sales. Keep in mind that the lids must be purchased new to ensure a tight seal.

- **Experiment with dehydration.** We bought our food dehydrator for $50 on Kijiji and have had so much fun experimenting with different fruits, vegetables, and herbs. From fruit leathers made from blended berries and apples to whole fruits like apricots and watermelon, dehydrating food can make your summer vegetables last through until spring. Whenever we have a bumper crop of tomatoes, we make sun-dried tomatoes and preserve them in olive oil. We dry any extra herbs and grind them up for homemade spice blends. Dried berries, grapes, bananas, and apples make delicious and healthful snacks.

Foodcycling

Foodcycling is quickly becoming a popular way for community members to share their abundance of fruits and vegetables with others. Maybe you have an abundance of apples from a big tree in your backyard, or you know of a great local spot to pick wild mulberries. Perhaps you have a bumper crop of pickling cucumbers, but could really use some black walnuts for your winter oatmeal. Foodcycling boards online or at community centres allow you to seek out specific foods from others or offer some of your own surplus for neighbours to enjoy. It's a fun and unique way to grow your winter stockpile and strengthen the food security of your local community.

Frugal Foundations

- **Explore community bulletin boards.** Check out your local community message boards or online garage sale sites like Kijiji, Craigslist, or Freecycle for foodcycling options in your area. We've all heard the anecdote of gardeners leaving zucchini on their neighbours' doorsteps because they grew more than they could possibly consume. These bulletin boards are essentially the same, with members offering or seeking surplus foodstuffs to share.

- **Ask your neighbours.** If you see a tree in a neighbour's yard that isn't being picked, consider asking if you can glean some of the fruit. Sometimes trees are owned by people who don't have the resources, time, or ability to maintain them. Instead of allowing the fruit to rot, my husband and I will typically ask if we can gather some of the fruit that has fallen to the ground. The owners are usually very happy that the food won't go to waste and will often allow us to take fruit directly from the trees as well. We will also offer to pick fruit for the owner if they are unable to do so themselves. Within our friend group, we also trade fruit for home-canned food, such as apples for apple butter or fresh cherries for pie filling. That way, the fruit isn't going to waste, and we all get something delicious and nutritious from the exchange.

- **Lead by example.** Stepping out of your comfort zone and welcoming shared food is an ideal way to promote frugality and sustainable living. If you have a surplus of produce, try foodcycling with others in your community. Post an ad on your local Freecycle or community message boards to offer some of your bounty to share. Another popular way for frugarians to share their surplus is by creating or donating to community food pantries—most often located outside community centres or places of worship. If there isn't one in your area, consider contacting your local community league to see if a small cupboard or storage chest could be installed.

Stockpiling

A stockpile is simply a collection of resources that you store up now to help provide for the future. While you can stockpile pretty much anything, frugarians tend to prioritize their needs and ensure their basic pantry staples are always well supplied before purchasing more specialty items. The size of your stockpile will depend on the size of your family, the amount of storage space in your home, and your budget.

Other than fresh groceries, we stockpile pretty much everything—non-perishable food, medicine and vitamins, personal hygiene items, cleaning supplies, toilet paper and paper towels, soaps and shampoos, bath towels and facecloths, kitchen towels and scrub brushes, plastic zipper bags, parchment paper and tin foil, cat food and litter, batteries—anything that we know we use in our household consistently. Stockpiling is not only good for emergency preparedness, but it also acts as a buffer against sudden financial challenges like an economic recession or job loss.

Frugal Foundations

- **Start your stockpile on any income.** No matter how much you have budgeted each month for food and household items, you can begin to stockpile. When I started out on my own after high school, I wasn't making much money. I was working a fast-food job and living paycheck to paycheck. I had just enough money to meet my basic needs, but not much left over at the end of each pay period. Even so, there were times when some items on my shopping list were on sale—and I came in a few dollars under budget. Whenever that happened, I would stock up on a couple of miscellaneous items. I would check the clearance bins for good deals and the weekly flyer for loss leaders to see how far I could stretch that money. Since those items weren't part of my weekly meal plan, they went right into the pantry to give me some added food security. I'd grab items like condensed cream of mushroom soup, canned beans, peanut butter, pasta sauce, and boxed macaroni and cheese. For non-food items, I'd stock up on dish detergent, toilet paper, and tissues.

- **Only purchase foods that you really eat.** Before Hubby and I met, he was faced with a job loss during the downturn of 2008. With a small budget, he grew his stockpile of canned goods to sustain him during those lean months. But some of the items he bought—including several cases of Chef Boyardee Ravioli— were not foods that he typically ate. After a couple of years in his pantry, he donated them to the local food bank. For families on a tight budget, it may seem like a good deal at the time to pick up those cheaper items, but it could end up costing you in the long run if you don't eat them.

- **Check grocery store flyers weekly for sales.** Most major grocery chains have online flyers, and many local stores deliver paper flyers right to your home. Each week, grocers offer a few major sales to entice shoppers into their stores. Since "loss leaders" are priced below cost, they're ideal for building your stockpile. Canned soups, vegetables, beans, tuna, rice, oatmeal, and pasta are popular loss leaders. You can grow your pantry a little at a time by consistently using your stockpiling budget on sale-priced items. We tend to check the flyers from several different stores and plan our weekly shopping trip based on which stores have the best deals.

- **Adopt seasonal stockpiling.** Have you ever noticed that condiments tend to go on sale during BBQ season, while packets of gravy and boxed stuffing are great deals around Thanksgiving and Christmas? That's because grocery stores mark down popular items around different seasonal holidays to maximize their profits. Paying attention to seasonal discounts is a frugal way to plan your stockpile purchases since certain items will be on sale at different times of the year. Winter holidays are the perfect time to stockpile baking supplies like flour, oats, baking powder, sugar, and vanilla. Fall is ideal for canned pumpkin and spices like cinnamon, cloves, and nutmeg. Non-food items can also be stockpiled seasonally. Summer is an excellent time to stock up on reusable containers and aluminum foil, while cleaning supplies often go on sale in the spring.

- **Aim for a six-month stockpile.** As a new frugarian, it may be overwhelming to think about long-term stockpiling and planning for emergencies. But aiming for a six-month stockpile is an important part of fighting inflation and preparing for unexpected hardships. While the process can be daunting when you consider the end goal, it can be easier to approach it as a series of smaller steps. When we were first building our stockpile as a family, we started with a one-week supply of non-perishable food, water, medical supplies and prescriptions, and any personal health and cleaning supplies we needed to keep ourselves and our home sanitary. By shopping for loss leaders each week, we gradually increased our stockpiled items into a six-month supply. Over the years, we have grown our stockpile to contain multiple years' worth of goods—which came in handy during the pandemic and also earlier last year when my husband lost his job and was without income for several months.

Part 8
Frugal Lifestyle

Companies around the world spend billions of dollars each year on consumer marketing. Through TV commercials, billboards, print advertisements, and social media, businesses sell their version of the ideal lifestyle—a way of living that can only be achieved by purchasing their products and services. But leading a frugal lifestyle means taking that marketing at face value and recognizing that life has so much more meaning than what items you bought from which stores and how much you spent.

Being a frugarian means understanding the power of persuasion and realizing that your needs can be met simply and affordably—regardless of what big brands and influencers try to make you believe. At the heart of frugality is authenticity and an intentionality to focus on what truly brings satisfaction and meaning to your life. It's about being proud of your choice to live frugally and releasing yourself from the perceptions and expectations of others.

Personal Hygiene

With social media influencers dominating the modern advertising space, many of us are bombarded with unrealistic (and expensive) expectations of how we're supposed to look and smell. One of the biggest examples of persuasive marketing lies in the personal hygiene space—items like shampoo, conditioner, soap, lotion, toothpaste, deodorant, shaving cream, and feminine hygiene products. They're necessary to keep us clean and feeling good about ourselves, but in most cases, the basic versions are just as effective as their designer counterparts. As a new frugarian, you can also make many personal hygiene items simply and cost-effectively by hand.

Frugal Foundations

- **Choose generic shampoo.** Generic shampoos are a smart option for the newly frugal because they offer the same essential cleansing benefits as name-brand versions at a fraction of the cost. Dollar stores and retail marts often carry low-priced basic shampoos, and it's not uncommon to see bottles of designer shampoos in the clearance section of the grocery store.

- **Cut conditioner with water.** To reduce the price of your favourite conditioner, pour half into a second bottle and fill the two bottles with water. Gently shake to combine. Most conditioners are very thick and don't lose their effectiveness when diluted with water.

- **Make your own soap.** If you're crafty and like to try new things, making your own soap can be a frugal way to both reduce the cost and improve the quality of your personal cleanser. As a beginner, you can purchase budget soapmaking kits online. When you're ready to expand your skills, you can start creating a variety of soaps on your own from scratch. Check out *Heartway Farms' Easy Homemade Soap* recipe on YouTube (18). Once you've perfected your technique, selling handmade soaps at craft fairs and farmers' markets can be a potential side hustle.

- **Embrace homemade hygiene products.** Smelling good and having fresh breath is easy as a frugarian with basic recipes for deodorant and toothpaste. *Wholehearted Eats* has an excellent recipe for *3 Ingredient Toothpaste* with coconut oil, baking soda, and oil of oregano (19). Making deodorant is similarly easy, with ingredients like beeswax, coconut oil, shea butter, and arrowroot powder. *House Full of Handmade* has a terrific recipe for a *Homemade Deodorant Stick* (20). Try making larger batches to stockpile your family's supply for the year.

- **Try a deodorant stone.** For a natural and frugal alternative to traditional stick-style deodorants, consider a deodorant stone. Made from potassium alum, a type of natural salt, deodorant stones have antimicrobial properties and can eliminate odours for up to 24 hours.

- **Explore options for sustainable feminine hygiene.** Up until the mid-1950s, most women wore reusable "rags" as their sanitary pads. They would soak the soiled cloths in a soap and bleach solution and launder them for repeated use. The modern version of reusable pads is growing in popularity—even outside of frugal circles—since they're affordable and promote environmentally conscious consumption. Etsy is a great resource for sustainable handmade cloth pads, but if you're handy with a sewing machine, they're simple to make for a fraction of the price. *Little House Living* has a free, easy-to-follow pattern for *Homemade Cloth Pads* (21). Another popular option is a menstrual cup—a small, reusable silicone cup that collects menstrual flow safely and sustainably.

Medicine and Prescriptions

It may feel counterintuitive to consider using frugal alternatives for medicine and prescriptions, since we tend to invest so much money into our overall wellness. Between the targeted advertisements and advice from your doctor, it's easy to be swayed towards manufactured remedies and name-brand drugs. But as a new frugarian, there are plenty of alternatives that can lead to major cost savings—not to mention the added health benefits of natural and holistic treatments.

Frugal Foundations

- **Consider natural remedies for minor ailments.** With the availability of over-the-counter (OTC) medications, it can be easy—even second nature—to reach for pharmaceuticals even when a natural substitute could be just as effective. When I was a teen, instead of giving me extra-strength ibuprofen for menstrual cramps, my mom would boil water and fill our trusty rust-coloured rubber bottle to rest on my tummy. Not only was it a natural treatment, but it was warm, comforting, and relaxing in a way that a little round pill never could be. As an adult, I default to seeking out more natural ways to feel better when I'm sick. Where I used to reach for cold and flu tablets and cough syrup for a sore throat and the sniffles, now I brew a pot of honey lemon tea or defrost a tub of my homemade batch-cooked chicken soup. Where I used to take medicine for back pain and sore joints, I now take long soaks in hot Epsom salt baths. Natural, frugal remedies often do more than just heal the body—they soothe the spirit and soul.

- **Choose generic prescriptions when available.** Prescription treatments for more serious medical conditions can be surprisingly expensive. Depending on your insurance plan, coverage limits, and co-pays, medications can eat up a huge chunk of your monthly budget. While some prescriptions are highly specialized and don't have generic alternatives, many common medications do—often at a fraction of the price. Personally, I take a biosimilar medication for ulcerative colitis and have saved hundreds of dollars each month by switching to the generic version. While I won't recommend specific drugs, I encourage you to speak with your doctor about safe, affordable generic alternatives to your current prescriptions.

- **Buy medication in bulk.** When I was in university, I started my first regular medication. Without giving it much thought, I would visit the pharmacy every month to renew my prescription. At the time, I didn't realize that each refill came with a dispensing fee—a small charge for counting, packaging, and labelling the medication. Even though it was only ten dollars per month, those fees added up over the year and were a noticeable expense for a struggling student. By switching to a multiple-month supply, I cut those costs way down. If your doctor approves a six-month prescription, for example, you'll only pay that fee twice per year instead of twelve times for a monthly renewal. The same applies to OTC medications, where buying in bulk is the frugal choice. A 500-count bottle of aspirin costs much less per pill than a 50-count version—and with their long shelf life, it's worth the upfront investment.

- **Batch cook homemade chicken soup.** When you have a cold or the flu, nothing quite hits the spot like a hot bowl of homemade soup. For generations, soups made from bones, aromatic vegetables, and herbs have been a natural and frugal way to bring vitamins, minerals, and collagen to ailing family members. They're delicious, affordable, and can easily be made in large batches and frozen for future meals—which is especially useful when you're under the weather. This timeless tradition helps restore strength, hydration, and energy when it's needed most. Our favourite recipe is the *Cold Fighting Chicken Noodle Soup* from *Damn Delicious* (22).

Frugal Fitness

There's a common misconception that you have to go to a gym and pay for a monthly membership to get fit and healthy. But that's simply not the case. If the last few years have shown us anything, it's that we're more than capable of finding alternative ways to stay active—and many of those methods are surprisingly frugal. While I still enjoy going to the gym once in a while, especially for group classes, I've found that working out at home is the most frugal and enjoyable option. Not only can you get a full-body session without leaving the house, but it's often easier and more comfortable because you're free from judgment and the self-consciousness that can come with exercising in public.

Frugal Foundations

- **Focus on exercise that doesn't cost money.** There are plenty of ways to stay active without spending a dime. You can take simple walks around your neighbourhood, follow along with free workout videos on YouTube, or download a no-cost app to guide you through circuit training right in your living room. If you prefer sports, try to pick activities without expensive memberships or costly equipment. For example, playing pick-up hockey means investing in pads, skates, helmets, sticks, and more, while basketball only requires a ball and a pair of running shoes—making it a much more frugal choice. My favourite workouts are with the old-school *Sweatin' to the Oldies* videos. Great soundtracks, adaptable for people with reduced mobility, and every time I'm out thrifting, I check the DVD section for more of Richard Simmons' beloved series to add to my collection.

- **Start collecting workout videos and DVDs.** Classic DVDs and videos often turn up at places like Goodwill or Savers, making them a fun and frugal way to add variety to your home exercise routine. You can often find popular titles like Billy Blanks' *Tae Bo*, Denise Austin's classic aerobics, Jillian Michaels' intense routines, or even *The Firm* series—all great options for different fitness levels and styles. Hunting for new titles while thrifting can be a fun little adventure, too. To keep things fresh, try swapping workout videos with friends and family. This switch-up gives you both new workouts to try without spending extra money. Plus, it's a great way to stay connected and motivated, even when you're exercising on your own.

- **Borrow workout videos from the library.** Libraries are a great place to discover a variety of fitness videos to match your specific interests—whether it's intense calisthenics, yoga flows, aerobics, or even exercises with your children. Since you can borrow as many videos as you want for free, you can easily change up your routine depending on your mood, the season, or your individual fitness goals.

- **Embrace walking.** One of the best exercises for your health is also one of the most frugal. Walking is an easy, low-cost way to enjoy a great workout. Whether you're heading out for a stroll around the block with your dog or meeting up with friends to walk through your local river valley or community park, it's a simple and effective way to stay fit. The only real expense is a good pair of shoes—and even those can often be found in like-new condition at thrift stores or for steep discounts during end-of-season sales. Walking is proof that staying active doesn't have to be expensive. Check out *MapMyWalk* for a free app to track your favourite routes.

- **Explore racket and ball sports.** Some of the most fun sports to play are also the most affordable. Basketball, volleyball, baseball, soccer, and football are all great frugal options—especially for kids and teens—because they don't require expensive gear. Most of the time, all you need is a ball and maybe a bat or a pair of rackets. These sports are also community-focused and team-oriented, without the constant expense of uniforms or protective equipment that needs to be replaced as kids grow. Balls and rackets often show up at garage sales and thrift shops, and if you invest in a ball pump, you can easily revive second-hand gear season after season instead of buying new.

Frugal Fashion

Like many aspects of frugal living, frugal fashion is often misunderstood. Some people assume that dressing on a budget means looking frumpy, outdated, or unkempt. Others believe that you have to sacrifice style or settle for last season's trends. In reality, frugal fashion is about intention—choosing clothes that make you feel good, reflect your personal style, and actually get worn in everyday life. It's about doing more with less and focusing on quality pieces that last year after year.

Frugal Foundations

- **Embrace a classic, traditional style.** Have you ever flipped through an old magazine and noticed how some outfits still look chic and timeless, even decades later? Or seen someone who looks effortlessly put together in the simplest clothes? That's the power of classic style. When you build your wardrobe around clean cuts, neutral tones, and timeless silhouettes—instead of chasing fast fashion trends—you get more wear out of every piece, and your look stays stylish long term. For inspiration, check out brands like Talbots or Ralph Lauren, known for their elegant, mix-and-match designs. Shopping end-of-season sales can lead to big savings, and I always head straight to the clearance section when buying clothing online. Some of my favourite classic pieces came from thrift stores, garage sales, and flea markets. If you're not sure where to start, try searching "Classic Style" on Pinterest for ideas.

- **Adopt a simple "uniform".** The most famous example of a uniform style was Steve Jobs, who stuck to his classic dark wash jeans, black turtleneck, and white sneakers to avoid wasting time deciding what to wear each day. He found that simplifying his wardrobe freed up mental energy for more important things. As a frugarian, you don't need to be that strict, but streamlining your style can bring big rewards in terms of time and money saved. You might even choose just one piece as your uniform—like Seattle blogger Alex Martin, who wore the same brown shift dress every day for a year. Her experiment reduced decision fatigue and laundry, and surprisingly, no one noticed she wore the same dress—she actually received numerous compliments on her effortless style! My daily uniform is comfortable black pants with pockets, a colourful t-shirt, and a coordinated cardigan. Simple, classic, and I can dress it up with accessories like scarves or different shoes.

- **Curate your capsule wardrobe.** Capsule wardrobes are popular among frugarians because they focus on just a few high-quality, timeless pieces that rarely go out of style. These versatile items can be mixed and matched to suit each season and occasion. Start by thinking about what you wear most and what you need—whether it's work clothes, casual wear, or special events. For example, if you rarely attend formal gatherings, one classic little black dress with different accessories can be worn for many years. If you only wear a suit for very special occasions, one well-fitting black or blue suit, paired with a couple of dress shirts and ties, can cover all your formal wear needs. A capsule wardrobe is all about investing in a few quality pieces that fit well and last, while still shopping frugally by hunting sales, thrift stores, or consignment shops. Check out *Pinch of Yum* for a guide for women on *How to Start a Capsule Wardrobe* (23), and *The Essential Man* for *How to Create a Capsule Wardrobe for Men* (24).

- **Make your own clothes or alter thrift-store finds.** If you're handy with a sewing machine or eager to learn, you can save a lot on your clothing budget by making your own garments. When I was young, my mom made clothes for us, from little romper dresses and simple coveralls to tunics and skirts as we got older. Sewing is quite approachable once you get the hang of it, and many of the most cost-saving pieces, like dresses and skirts, have simple, beginner-friendly patterns. You can also try "thrift-flipping" or buying imperfect thrift-store clothing and altering it to better fit your style and body. For helpful tutorials and ideas, check out *Coolirpa* on YouTube for sewing basics and thrift-flip inspiration (25).

- **Mend before you spend.** Have you ever ripped a favourite piece of clothing and immediately tossed it in the garbage or donation pile, thinking it was beyond repair? Or worn a favourite item so much that it became threadbare at the bum, crotch, inner thighs, or elbows—and then given up on it? In today's disposable, consumer-driven culture, it's much easier to replace rather than repair. But as a frugarian, your mindset should shift to finding ways to make your worn clothes feel like new again. Whether you learn to mend them yourself or take them to a local tailor, repairing garments usually costs far less than buying new. With a bit of practice, you can handle simple repairs by hand using just thread, a needle, and some time.

Another popular trend is "visible mending", where the repair is more like embroidery and part of the style. Take a look at *Visible Mending: 10 Basic Principles to Get You Started Mending Your Clothes* by *Stuart Moores Textiles* on YouTube for beginner mending techniques (26).

- **Buy or sell clothing at consignment stores.** I've found some great pieces at consignment stores over the years—everything from name-brand basics to rare vintage items I wouldn't have found anywhere else. If you're looking to buy high-quality or designer garments, you can often find them at a fraction of the retail price. And when you need to clear out your closet, consignment shops are a smart way to earn a little money back on gently used items. After my wedding, I took my dress to the consignment store and made almost half of the original cost back—all while giving another frugarian a beautiful budget dress for her big day.

- **Do a "clothing swap" with friends and family.** One of my favourite annual traditions within my social group is hosting a clothing swap. It's a fun, low-pressure way for everyone to clean out their closets and find something new to them without spending any money. The host invites everyone over and asks them to bring their unwanted garments and their favourite snack to share. You can run the swap however you like: hold up each piece and let people call dibs, or throw everything into a big pile for a silly, free-for-all treasure hunt. It's always a blast, and at the end of the night, everyone leaves with something fresh for their wardrobe. Anything left behind can be donated to a local thrift store or shelter.

- **Take care of and repair your shoes.** Shoes are typically a big part of your clothing budget, so it's important to get the most value and wear out of them as you can. Strive to purchase quality leather shoes with thick soles and a patterned tread. You can keep a rag by the door and wipe off water or dirt right after coming inside to protect the leather and keep it strong. A simple shoe-shine kit and a quick polish a few times a year can make your shoes last a long time—I have boots I've worn for 10 years that still look great thanks to regular care. Keep in mind that thrift stores often have quality footwear that just needs a little cleaning and fresh laces. If your shoes are damaged beyond what polish and a buff can repair, taking them to a local cobbler is a smart, frugal alternative to buying new.

- **Wash clothing in cold water.** Laundering clothes in tap-cold water is a frugal double whammy: it saves you money on heated water and extends the life of your garments by preserving colour and minimizing pilling and shrinkage.

- **Use the dryer to fluff line-dried items.** There's nothing better than slipping into a warm shirt or pants fresh out of the dryer, but running your load through a full dryer cycle can lead to pilling, fading, and shrinkage. When the weather allows, try hanging your clothing on an outdoor clothesline and use the dryer just to fluff them up once they're nearly dry. This frugal practice not only saves money on your utility bill, but also helps your garments last longer—so you spend less money replacing items that look old before they're worn out.

- **Accessorize to add variety to your look.** One of the easiest and most affordable ways to add variety to a capsule wardrobe is through accessories. Scarves, ties, necklaces, and belts can completely change the feel of an outfit, depending on your mood or style preferences in the moment. Personally, I wear the same black cardigan to work most days, but I switch up the scarf I pair with it. It keeps my look fresh and adds a pop of colour—without needing a closet full of clothes. I'm always on the lookout at thrift stores for unique scarves to add to my collection. I rarely pay more than a dollar or two per scarf, and I keep an eye on tag sales at Goodwill to score the best deals. A few well-chosen accessories can go a long way in refreshing your wardrobe and making it feel larger and more diverse.

- **Take care of what you have.** Caring for your clothes extends their life and maximizes their value. Small actions—like treating stains immediately, mending tears before they worsen, washing clothes inside out, and storing them properly—can make a big impact on your clothing budget. By treating your wardrobe like an investment, you'll start to see that the time spent maintaining your garments is far less than the time and effort required to earn the money to buy an item brand new. When I tore my pant leg on a sharp bit of metal on an exterior door at work, I was annoyed because they were my favourite! But instead of throwing them in the trash or cutting them up for rags, I took 15 minutes, a piece of strong black thread, and a needle—and saved them. I still wear those pants two years later, and you can't even tell where the rip was.

Hair and Beauty

Individual expenses for hair and beauty products may not be the biggest line items in your budget, but the costs can add up quickly—especially when you factor in high-end products, frequent salon visits, and ever-changing trends. The core principles of modesty, minimalism, and intentional living are at the heart of a frugal lifestyle and often extend into how we approach our personal presentation and grooming. Embracing a simpler, more natural routine doesn't mean sacrificing self-care—it means scaling back and appreciating the true meaning of beauty.

Frugal Foundations

- **Cut your own hair.** When I was younger with poker-straight hair, I endured my fair share of bowl cuts. Those blunt, uneven snips were a common sight in my grade school classroom when the mid-eighties recession was in full swing. At that time, it made more financial sense for mothers to cut their children's hair than to take them to even the cheapest strip mall salons. As I aged, my hair became curly, which has made it even easier to give myself "twist and snip" trims. With this method, I twist small sections of hair into long, quarter-inch-thick ropes, then cut about two inches off the end of each twist. I've been using this technique every six months for years. For a great visual guide, check out *Pick Up Limes* on YouTube for *How I Cut & Layer My Hair at Home* (27). Haircuts for men and boys can be even simpler, especially with a classic buzz cut. With a decent pair of clippers and a bit of practice, you can get professional-looking results at home. For guidance, visit the *Buzz Cut Guide* for tips on *How to Cut Your Own Hair* (28).

- **Try a low-maintenance hairstyle.** Anyone who's ever had short hair knows it comes with a side order of trims every 6 to 8 weeks. This recurring cost might be worth keeping in your budget if you truly love your short style or need a polished, professional look for work. But if you're open to something different, consider a cut that only needs attention a few times a year. For women, a mid-length bob is a timeless option—for men, a simple buzz cut keeps things neat without frequent trips to the barber.

- **Embrace going gray.** One of the most empowering trends in the frugal living community is going gray naturally. Like many people, I experimented with a lot of different hair colours in my youth—as a frugarian, I always opted for drugstore boxed colour. But by the time I reached my mid-twenties, I was dyeing it several times per year to cover up the roots. After a few years of battling the realities of getting older, I decided to give up the colour and go gray. I not only saved money and time, but I also eliminated my exposure to those harsh chemicals. I also gained confidence because I was no longer worried about whether my roots were showing. Check out *Katie Goes Platinum* (29) for tips on how to gracefully transition your hair to natural gray.

- **Go makeup-free.** With celebrities like Alicia Keys and Pamela Anderson embracing a makeup-free lifestyle, this longtime frugal practice is gaining popularity among women worldwide. While some frugarians shop sales or wear minimal makeup to cut costs, nothing is more frugal than not wearing it at all. Makeup isn't just expensive—it often contains harmful chemicals and is typically tested on animals. Going makeup-free can also improve your skin's health and appearance. Many frugal women rave about looking younger without makeup, which tends to emphasize fine lines and wrinkles around the eyes and mouth. Check out *Fine Fit Day* for practical tips on *How to Rock NO Makeup* (30).

- **Embrace minimalist makeup.** Let's face it: makeup is expensive. Between concealer, primer, foundation, powder, blush, bronzer, shadow, liner, mascara, and lipstick, you could easily spend $50 a month for a daily face of makeup—and that doesn't even include the makeup removers, lotions, toners, and creams you need to prep your skin for the next day. Natural makeup looks are *naturally* frugal since they use less product by enhancing your existing features and allowing your beauty to shine through instead of masking it. Check out *Minimalism Made Simple* for minimalist makeup tips (31).

Part 9
Frugal Fulfillment

If I were to poll 100 people and ask what makes them feel truly fulfilled, how many do you think would say money? How many would mention a house, a car, nice clothes, fancy trips, or loads of vacation time? And how many would say their contentment comes simply from knowing that their family's basic needs are met?

For me, fulfillment comes from my relationships with family and the creative work I love—writing, photography, and art. Does having more money in the bank make me more fulfilled? It certainly brings a greater sense of security, but the real fulfillment comes from knowing that my family is nurtured and supported. Living a frugal lifestyle and being debt-free gives me the mental clarity to appreciate what I have, to focus on meaningful moments with loved ones, and to experience creative joy and expression.

Take a moment to consider what brings you fulfillment without a price tag. Maybe it's the satisfaction of doing a good job and receiving praise at work. Maybe it's the indulgent pleasure of popping a sheet of bubble wrap and feeling the little explosions of air between your fingers. Perhaps it's seeing the smile on your child's face when the dog curls up in their lap for a nap. As you embrace a frugal lifestyle, your connection to these small moments will deepen, giving you a clearer understanding of what truly matters. Trust me—it's rarely "stuff".

Faith

Embracing your faith community is one of the most meaningful and cost-effective ways to experience deep fulfillment. It grounds you spiritually, connects you with others who share your values, and provides a supportive network through both the joyful and challenging seasons of life. Many faith-based activities are naturally frugal—potlucks, park gatherings, and volunteer-led events offer rich social and spiritual experiences without financial strain. Beyond that, integrating faith into your daily habits fosters peace, purpose, and resilience—especially during times of financial uncertainty.

Frugal Foundations

- **Prioritize connection over entertainment.** Instead of spending money on restaurants, movies, or outings that quickly add up, seek connection through shared meals and gatherings within your faith community. Host a potluck after weekly services or invite a few friends over for coffee and conversation. These moments build community, encourage hospitality, and remind you that true joy comes from relationships—not receipts. Since communal meals are a common way to connect, start collecting tried-and-true frugal recipes that are easy to prepare and appeal to a wide range of people. Check out Julia Pacheco on YouTube for amazing budget-friendly casseroles and other potluck-friendly meal ideas (32).
- **Open your home as a gathering place.** Bringing people together in your home builds community and supports spiritual growth with few added expenses. Hosting prayer meetings, study groups, or worship gatherings at home creates a warm, welcoming space while saving money on transportation, childcare, and event costs. Simple touches—like lighting a candle or

serving fragrant tea—help set a peaceful, inviting atmosphere for your guests. If meeting in person is a challenge, platforms like Zoom offer free, easy-to-use options for virtual gatherings.

- **Contribute in your own way.** Giving and charity are important parts of many faith traditions, but they don't have to strain your budget. When I was going through a tough financial situation, I could only afford to give about $5 per week to the charity food bank. During that time, I found other meaningful ways to contribute—by volunteering in the kitchen during events, helping with cleanup, and running errands. These acts of service are just as valuable as monetary gifts and can often be even more appreciated (and rewarding). Remember, no one expects you to give more than you can afford. Your willingness to contribute however you can is what truly matters.

- **Participate in skill-sharing activities.** Faith communities bring together people with a wide range of talents. From sewing and budgeting to using a computer or preserving food, sharing your knowledge with others is an inspired way to foster self-reliance and frugality. One of my skills is baking, and I often print copies of a recipe when I bring treats to share. Other members organize workshops, skill-sharing events, or "teach-and-share" evenings throughout the year. These small acts of sharing help create a faith community that is more connected, resourceful, and resilient.

- **Lean on faith during hardships.** Frugality often begins out of necessity, but it can be sustained through purpose. Whether facing job loss, health issues, or major life transitions, faith can provide hope and stability beyond what money can buy. Set aside time daily for prayer, reflection, or reading sacred texts, and connect with your faith community for support. By grounding your frugal lifestyle in faith, you're not just saving money—you're building a life centred on what matters most: community, compassion, generosity, and peace. Even simple acts, like sharing a meal or welcoming a neighbour, take on deeper meaning when you give of yourself despite personal challenges.

Family

For many of us, the relationships closest to our hearts are the ones we share with family. We might not always agree or get along perfectly, but the bonds we hold with relatives are deep and enduring—and are also occasionally overlooked in the rush of everyday life. Adopting a frugal lifestyle helps clear mental and physical clutter, giving us the time and presence to truly engage with loved ones.

I often think back to my childhood in the "MTV generation". We didn't have money for video game consoles, fancy toys, or elaborate outings, so I spent most afternoons and weekends at my grandmother's house nearby. We'd sit at her kitchen table, sipping overly sweet Red Rose tea and playing card games like rummy, Go Fish, or cribbage. We laughed, competed, and shared stories—turning simple moments into lasting memories. Those afternoons with Grammy remain far richer in my mind than any screen or high score ever could.

Frugal Foundations

- **Make family time your most valuable resource.** You don't need elaborate outings or expensive vacations to connect with family. What matters is showing up and being fully present, without distraction. Carve out moments to play games, cook together, work on a puzzle, or just sit and talk. Hubby and I make a point to connect each Saturday over coffee and a home-cooked breakfast—a simple, frugal ritual that lets us check in with each other and disconnect from the work week. These small, intentional moments often become the memories your children, partner, and family cherish most.

- **Start frugal traditions that bring you together.** Simple, consistent rituals often have the greatest impact. Once a month, Hubby and I head to the library together, hunting for foreign or indie films to borrow. Wandering the aisles, chatting over forgotten favourites, and discovering hidden gems has become a much-anticipated adventure. Other low-cost traditions— Sunday strolls, cooking a new recipe together, or backyard stargazing—can grow into touchstones of connection over time. It's the shared experience, not the spending, that makes them meaningful and memorable.

- **Tell your stories and listen to theirs.** Some of our most treasured moments happen when we trade stories with family members. You can share your own memories, ask elders about their youth, and encourage kids to share tales of their schoolyard adventures. I'll never forget my grandpa telling us the story of finding a box of frozen ice cream treats with his brother outside a corner store in the 1930s. It had been forgotten by the deliveryman and was at risk of melting. He and my great uncle each ate six ice cream bars—and got very ill. The memory of my grandpa telling the story still makes me laugh! Sharing stories like this was how my grandpa and I could still have meaningful conversations even during his deepest dementia. Moments like these remind us that presence and connection are priceless.

- **Bond through shared effort.** Frugal households thrive on collaboration, and working together often becomes its own form of connection. Hubby and I alternate who cooks supper, turning meal prep into a small, enjoyable routine. We often spend weekends in the garden helping each other plant, weed, or harvest, and team up with family members for handyman projects like painting, landscaping, or mending fences. These tasks lighten the load, encourage teamwork, and create a sense of pride in what we accomplish together. Children especially love pitching in, and you'll be surprised at how much intimacy is created while snapping beans, baking bread, or folding laundry side by side. The work itself becomes part of the memory, with the process as rewarding as the results.

Friends

Hubby and I have a small circle of like-minded friends. Rather than meeting for fancy dinners or $8 lattes at coffee shops, we host backyard fires to roast weenies or take walks together in our local parklands. We invite each other over for tea and homemade baked goods, or host movie nights with fresh buttered popcorn. Golf is another favourite pastime, so we head to the driving range or meet up for casual games of "pitch-and-putt", saving the expensive 18-hole courses for a couple of times each summer. Our friends understand that our focus is on spending time together, not spending money. I remember one summer evening when we brought a box of vegetables from our garden to a friend's house—the excitement, conversation, and shared generosity made it far more memorable than any night out at a chain restaurant. Being open about our frugal lifestyle naturally encourages invitations toward meaningful, affordable experiences that focus on shared moments instead of consumption.

Frugal Foundations

- **Spend time, not money.** When you focus on togetherness instead of outings, the pressure to spend fades—and what's left is real intimacy. Last fall, Hubby and I invited a few close friends over for a games night. We brewed a pot of decaf coffee, pulled my famous chocolate chip cookies from the freezer, and laughed and cheered each other on while playing our favourites. Those simple, intentional moments created memories far richer than an expensive night out at a restaurant or pub.

- **Be upfront and honest about your lifestyle.** You don't need to give a big explanation for why you're frugal—just be open in everyday situations. At my previous job, I mentioned to coworkers that I'd love to join them for coffee once a week instead of every day. It quickly became a relaxed Friday tradition we all looked forward to. We'd chat, laugh, and catch up without the pressure of a daily expense or time commitment. When you set financial boundaries kindly and confidently, people usually respect them—and many are quietly relieved to let go of the same pressure.

- **Seek out others who live simply.** Spending time with friends who value simplicity makes frugal living feel natural instead of restrictive. Local garden clubs, thrift store volunteering, or online groups are great places to start forming friendships. My closest friends are the ones who love potlucks, upcycling, handmade fibre-arts, and homegrown produce. When we spend time together, we never run out of things to talk about and are always learning something new from each other. When your values align, friendships tend to run deeper and feel effortless.

- **Choose thoughtful gestures over costly ones.** Showing you care doesn't have to mean buying gifts or paying for outings. A handwritten note, repotted seedlings from your garden, or a batch of homemade soup can mean just as much—often even more. These small, thoughtful gestures cost very little but carry a lot of meaning. They deepen friendships in a way money rarely can.

- **Prioritize experiences that foster real conversation.** The most treasured moments between friends can happen without the burden or pressure to spend. One of my favourite memories is when a coworker and I decided to skip the busy local lunch spots and have a picnic across the street instead. We each brought food from home, found a shady table, and spent our break laughing and talking about life beyond deadlines and office obligations. It cost next to nothing, yet the conversation felt rich and meaningful.

Community

One of the most powerful and rewarding parts of living a frugal lifestyle is the sense of community that comes with it. Sharing your frugal experiences, such as mending clothing, downsizing your home, or hosting a DIY wedding, helps you lead by example and draw like-minded people into your circle. Frugality isn't just about spending less—it's about living more intentionally and supporting each other along the way. There are frugarians in every community, often quietly building networks of support, skill-sharing, and mutual generosity. When you step into that world, you'll find more than just money-saving tips—you'll find meaning.

Frugal Foundations

- **Lead by example.** Frugality is best shared when it's lived authentically, not preached. I've lost count of the number of conversations sparked by a thrifted outfit, a pot of homemade soup, or a lush backyard garden. Curiosity grows naturally when people see practical, joyful frugality in real life—whether it's meal-prepping with homegrown vegetables, repairing an item instead of replacing it, or visiting the library to gather entertainment for the week. When you practice frugality openly, you teach others through your actions.

- **Join a local barter or Freecycle network.** I once attended a backyard wedding where nearly everything—from linens to lights—was borrowed from friends and family. The simple celebration was proof that, with a frugal mindset and a supportive community, you can create extraordinary debt-free experiences. That same bartering spirit fuels clothing swaps, tool-lending libraries, carpools, Freecycle groups, and bulk-buying clubs. Before I relocated for university, I downsized my wardrobe by posting "Free Bag of Women's Clothing" on Kijiji. Within hours, a local woman picked it up and thanked me so much for sharing. A couple of years later, when I wanted to dry fresh herbs from our garden, a family on a Freecycle website gave their old dehydrator to us. You don't need a big network to start—even a neighbourhood swap meet or Facebook post can spur connections and pave the way for a thriving barter community.

- **Get involved in your local community league.** Neighbour-hood associations and community leagues are hidden gems for frugarians. In my city, most neighbourhoods have a rental hall, parkland, playground, sports field, and even an open-air skating rink. These hubs host free or low-cost events like flea markets, craft sales, cribbage nights, and outdoor concerts. One of the most rewarding parts of my frugal journey has been walking through my residential area and recognizing familiar faces—honestly, it reminds me of *Mister Rogers' Neighborhood*. There's something special about getting to know the people you share space with. Volunteering or participating in local activities helps you connect with neighbours and fosters a sense of place and belonging. This can be especially fulfilling for children, since the friendships they build with other kids in their community can last a lifetime.

- **Create a culture of generosity.** Frugal living becomes more joyful when it's shared. Lending out your slow cooker, passing along books you've finished, or gifting surplus tomatoes isn't just kind—it builds trust and relationships. Helping others in any way you can creates a quiet but powerful system of mutual support. Over time, people return the favour, and an informal economy of generosity and reciprocity begins to flourish. Small acts—like baking muffins for a neighbour, shovelling a sidewalk, or swapping homemade soup for fresh herbs—show that frugal living is about building abundance together.

The Obligation of Gifting

As part of your newly frugal lifestyle, consider stepping back from the "gift" culture that often defines modern celebrations. Many holidays today feel more commercial than meaningful. In our home, we've chosen to focus on connection instead of consumption. We still celebrate birthdays, but with things like a homemade breakfast, a walk together, or a handmade card instead of purchased gifts. If you still enjoy giving, keep it simple and useful—a thrifted find, a homemade treat, or something crafted by hand. One of my favourite frugal gifts to share is a jar of homemade cookie mix tucked into a second-hand jar with a handwritten recipe. These kinds of gestures remind us that the real value of giving comes from thought and care, not from the amount spent.

Frugal Foundations

- **Create experiences instead of piles of stuff.** Rather than giving physical gifts, focus on experiences that bring warmth and connection. A few years ago, instead of buying Hubby a present,

I cooked him a full steakhouse-style dinner—butcher counter steaks, buttery garlic bread, and a homemade Caesar salad with fresh bacon bits. It was simple, intimate, and memorable. Experiences like these often linger in the heart far longer than anything that comes in a gift bag.

- **Take advantage of once-loved finds.** You would be amazed at the giftable items you can find second-hand. One year, I scored a new marble cutting board at a thrift shop and later paired it with a silver-plated cheese knife I'd picked up at a garage sale. I wrapped them together with a few fine cheeses and a colourful tea towel for a "foodie" friend. It looked beautiful, felt personal, and carried real consideration. Gifts like these show care and creativity without relying on brand-new items. Check out *Tasha at Home* on YouTube for thoughtful thrifted gift ideas (33).

- **Gift from the heart with homemade goods.** There's something deeply personal about a gift made by hand. It doesn't have to be elaborate—hand-mixed spice blends, knitted scarves, or jars of preserves can all carry genuine meaning. One year, I spent my evenings crocheting a blanket for my mother, stitch by stitch. It took time, but every moment felt like a quiet act of love. She still has it, and every time she uses it, she remembers that care. These small, crafted gestures are lasting ways to show our loved ones appreciation.

- **Celebrate through everyday acts of kindness.** True giving rarely comes wrapped in paper with a bow. Over time, I've learned that being helpful can be a gift in itself—cooking a meal, offering encouragement, or taking on a task for someone who's overwhelmed. These small gestures build deeper connections and lasting gratitude. When giving becomes an act of care instead of consumption, every day holds the potential for generosity.

Part 10
Frugal for Life

Now that you've learned the tools and mindset of a newly frugal lifestyle, it's time to take what resonates and make it your own. You don't have to do everything perfectly or all at once. Maybe you'll dive in fully, or maybe you'll start with one small shift—packing lunch more often, repairing something instead of replacing it, or saying "no" to an unnecessary purchase. Every consistent choice begins to change the way you see the world and how you function frugally within it.

Frugality isn't about restriction—it's about awareness. It's learning to pause before you spend, taking time to value what you already have, and freeing your mind to concentrate on building a life that feels rich in ways money can't buy. The goal isn't perfection but steadiness. Choosing simplicity over excess and thoughtfulness over impulse becomes easier over time and gradually feels natural.

Surrounding yourself with people who share a frugal mindset helps more than you might expect. When you deliberately live your values—mending, reusing, cooking from scratch, or finding joy in free experiences—others notice. Before long, you may find a small community forming around you. You may start to trade garden harvests, share tools, swap ideas, and learn new skills together. It's not about convincing anyone to live differently—it's about living intentionally in a way that quietly inspires.

Frugality isn't a phase or a challenge to "complete". It's a lifelong philosophy that deepens with practice. The more you lean into it, the more your priorities shift—from things to experiences, transactions to relationships, and spending to sharing. Over time, your life fills up with gratitude, creativity, and peace instead of *stuff.*

Frugal Foundations

- **Start small.** Tiny, steady changes add up faster than big, dramatic ones. Begin with simple habits like packing lunch more often, repairing instead of replacing, or skipping an unnecessary purchase. Over time, these small actions reshape your perspective and build lasting frugal habits. Focus on consistency instead of perfection to avoid becoming over-whelmed, and celebrate small victories along the way.

- **Treat frugality as a mindset, not a rulebook.** Frugality is rooted in thoughtfulness, not deprivation. Changing the spending and saving habits you've carried for a lifetime takes time, but the best place to start is with your mindset around money. Pause before buying, think about what you truly need, and look for ways to repurpose or reuse what you already own. These small mental shifts—seeing your lifestyle and purchases through a frugal lens—make it easier to choose function over instant gratification. As you ease into a more frugal way of living, be gentle with yourself. No one expects you to change overnight, and that isn't the goal.

- **Focus on family.** Prioritize time and experiences with the special people in your life. Shared meals, walks, or family projects create lasting memories that no amount of stuff can replace. Through daily frugal living, take opportunities to ask questions of elders who may have a thing or two to teach about saving pennies, doing without, and getting creative with what they had when times got tough. Lead by example with children and teenagers, showing how frugal acts like budgeting, shopping sales, and home cooking can set them up for financial stability in the future.

- **Enrich your life with experiences.** Seek joy and meaning through shared experiences rather than possessions. Choose activities that invite connection—walk a new trail together, visit a museum on a free-admission day, or pack a simple picnic to enjoy at a local park. Make traditions out of the little things, like Sunday morning coffee, seasonal decorating with what you already have, or watching classic movies as a family. Over time, these ordinary shared moments quietly become the foundation of a fulfilling life.

- **Find your circle.** Community keeps you encouraged, supported, and inspired. Connect with like-minded people who share similar values—neighbours who share tools, friends who exchange garden produce, or coworkers who enjoy learning practical skills together. Attend local meetups, thrift-store events, library workshops, or online groups, and grow your frugal foundation together.

- **Care for what you have.** Repair, reuse, and tend to your belongings—they'll last longer and serve you better. Simple acts like patching clothes, cleaning tools, or preserving food reduce waste and save money, while also creating a sense of satisfaction in what you own. Take time to maintain your home, appliances, and vehicles, and you'll be rewarded with reliability and longevity. Repurpose items creatively—turn old jars into storage or upcycle furniture with a fresh coat of paint. Even small, mindful acts like oiling wooden utensils or properly storing seasonal clothing contribute to a more intentionally frugal way of life.

- **Measure wealth in meaning.** Frugality frees you to focus on what truly matters: peace, purpose, and connection. Instead of measuring success by the things you own, pay attention to the moments and relationships that enrich your life. Spend time with loved ones, pursue creative hobbies, volunteer, or explore your community. By prioritizing experiences, relationships, and intentional living over consumption, you cultivate a life that feels genuinely rich, balanced, and deeply satisfying.

Living frugally isn't about denying yourself joy. It's about discovering it in the simplicity of everyday—in quiet mornings with coffee brewed at home, in shared meals with friends or family, in the contentment of knowing you have enough, and in the satisfaction of providing for your loved ones.

At its heart, frugality is gratitude in action. The more you practice it, the more you may recognize the truth in Henry David Thoreau's words: *"Simplify your life…live deep and suck out all the marrow of life"*.

A simple life, lived well, is a life of true abundance.

References

(1) The Federal Reserve. *2025 Diary of Consumer Payment Choice*, 2025.

(2) Oxford Languages, 2021.

(3) United States Environmental Protection Agency. *Facts and Figures on Materials, Wastes and Recycling*, 2018.

(4) Mental Health Commission of Canada, 2018.

(5) U.S. Census Bureau. *Who Can Afford To Live in a Home?* 2006.

(6) Consumer Credit Society, 2017.

(7) Credit Canada. *How Much Money You Should Spend on Monthly Expenses?* 2019.

(8) The 7 Baby Steps. Dave Ramsey. https://www.ramseysolutions.com/dave-ramsey-7-baby-steps

(9) U.S. Department of Transportation. *Summary of Travel Trends - 2022 National Household Travel Survey*, 2022.

(10) Family Handyman. https://www.youtube.com/@thefamilyhandyman

(11) College Board. *Trends in College Pricing 2024 Report*, 2024.

(12) The Canadian Press. *Household debt-to-income ratio ticked higher in Q2: Statistics Canada*, 2025.

(13) American Bankers Association Banking Journal. *New York Fed: Total household debt nearly $18.4 trillion in Q2*, 2025.

(14) Food Waste in the Home. https://lovefoodhatewaste.ca/about/food-waste/

(15) Food Banks Canada Hunger Count. https://foodbankscanada.ca/hungercount/

(16) The Quaint Housewife. www.youtube.com/@TheQuaintHousewife

(17) The Seedkeepers. www.youtube.com/@theseedkeepers105

(18) Heartway Farms. *Easy Homemade Soap.* www.youtube.com/watch?v=ZtU7GUebvzY

(19) Wholehearted Eats. *3 Ingredient Toothpaste.* www.wholeheartedeats.com

(20) Houseful of Handmade. *Homemade Deodorant Stick.* www.housefulofhandmade.com

(21) Little House Living. *Homemade Cloth Pads.* https://www.littlehouseliving.com/homemade-cloth-pads-tutorial-and-pattern.html

(22) Damn Delicious. *Cold Fighting Chicken Noodle Soup.* https://damndelicious.net/2018/09/30/cold-fighting-chicken-noodle-soup/

(23) Pinch of Yum. *How to Start a Capsule Wardrobe*. www.pinchofyum.com

(24) The Essential Man. *How to Create a Capsule Wardrobe for Men*. www.theessentialman.com

(25) Coolirpa. *Thrift Flips*. www.youtube.com/@coolirpa

(26) Stuart Moores Textiles. *Visible Mending: 10 Basic Principles to Get You Started Mending Your Clothes*. www.youtube.com/@stuartmoorestextiles

(27) Pick Up Limes. *How I Cut & Layer My Hair at Home*. https://www.youtube.com/@PickUpLimes

(28) The Buzzcut Guide. *How to Cut Your Own Hair*. www.buzzcutguide.com

(29) Katie Goes Platinum. www.katiegoesplatinum.com

(30) Fine Fit Day. *How to Rock NO Makeup*. www.finefitday.com

(31) Minimalism Made Simple. www.minimalismmadesimple.com

(32) Julia Pacheco. www.youtube.com/@JuliaPacheco

(33) Tasha at Home. www.youtube.com/@TashaatHome

Resources

LinkedIn Learning: https://www.linkedin.com/learning
edX: https://www.edx.org
Coursera: https://www.coursera.org
Alison: https://alison.com/
Emergency Kit List: https://www.ready.gov/kit
YouTube: https://www.youtube.com/
Tubi: https://tubitv.com/
Pinterest: https://ca.pinterest.com/
MapMyWalk: https://www.mapmywalk.com/
Zoom: https://www.zoom.com

About the Author

Lindsay Ripplinger is a professional writer, editor, and digital publisher based in Edmonton, Alberta, Canada. A trained archivist and storyteller, she writes essays, poetry, creative nonfiction, and fiction, often exploring the complexities of how the present reflects the past while shaping the future. Her literary historical fiction novel, *Seven Springs*, is published under the nom de plume Lindsay Shayne.

Lindsay brings curiosity, insight, and a love of practical problem-solving to a wide range of creative disciplines. She enjoys artisan collage, painting, singing, and photography, finding inspiration and beauty in the simple, everyday details of Alberta life. Drawing on her experiences with frugal living, she offers guidance that is thoughtful, practical, and relatable.